Protecting Kids Online!
Keeping Them Safe from Perverts, Stalkers, Data Thieves and Scammers

BY
Trip Elix llc
Consultant•Speaker•Author
Security Analyst

Publishing

For information about this title or to order other books and/or electronic media,
contact the publisher:
ww.tripelix.com

Paperback
ISBN 978-0-9915685-7-4
Hard cover
ISBN 978-0-9915685-4-3
Ebook
ISBN 978-0-9915685-8-1
Audiobook
ISBN 978-0-9915685-9-8

First Edition
Manufactured worldwide

Edited by
First Editing   www.FirstEditing.com

Acknowledgments

This book is dedicated to the children of America and to their future.

A special thanks to the divine spirit mystery of the universe, for letting there be music, children and laughter. Barb Early, who sparked more than an idea, and gave guidance and a direction to what would work and what would not. Jackson, Juliette and Kristina you will be living in a time when all of this changes and I hope that it will be a brighter world. So many of my personal friends, and those who made suggestions though this process, without you this would not have been possible. Nelly, Lori, Patrick, Linda and Frank who have always supported my efforts. And a special thank you to Donna, Trish and Dottie for giving their aid and their input.

This is a Promotional copy of Protecting Children Online! If you have any questions comments or concerns please call 413 248 7475

Table of Contents

Introduction

The children of today are being robbed of their childhoods. We are told that the internet never forgets and that is particularly true on the social networks. A simple error in judgment can be rebroadcast to millions of people in seconds. Part of being a child is about learning from mistakes. Many parents would never leave their child alone in a park or a mall but often will leave them on the internet with little or no supervision.

I believe strongly that personal security and privacy are interlinked. Without privacy, you cannot have personal security. It is that lack of personal security that we have today that makes identity theft seem out of control. In the following chapters, you will discover how to build not only a strategic defense but how you can leverage the internet to your child's advantage.

While the internet offers a universe of knowledge and connections to the larger world, it also poses risks for children beyond what most caregivers are accustomed to monitoring. Moreover, we are increasingly aware of the consequences of children's online actions to their caregivers and families.

While understanding the internet may seem beyond the reach of most ordinary people, I strongly believe caregivers should not accept this conclusion. I have been hearing this garbage since the second personal computer was invented that "technology moves so fast." The only thing that moves fast is the adoption of new applications. The way that most things work has changed very little in the last thirty years.

It is easy to understand it enough to help yourself and your children. There is key knowledge including some basic information about the internet, the types of activities that pose a risk to children and some steps that caregivers can take to protect their children, themselves, and the entire family.

I am highly involved with the technical side of the internet. I have spent many years working with individuals, families, businesses, and corporations on all aspects of computer and internet technology. I have written books regarding threats to personal information and identity on the internet and am especially insightful in explaining the challenges faced by children and families online. I believe that I can help caregivers to better understand the internet as well as their children's online behavior and steps to take towards safer usage.

The internet is not a game. It is not a safe means of anything. If it were even somewhat safe, you wouldn't hear the news filled with hacking or data breaches. For two generations, our children have grown up with the internet and experience a world of constant corporate surveillance. The risk of becoming an identity theft statistic starts at younger and younger ages.

Our schools are following suit with the rest of corporate America in the lie that big data provides any sort of reliable predictive human behavior. Big data and its lists of behavior are openly sold. Thus your child's name and address along with many other intimate details are for sale, to any criminal, predator, or another type of monster the internet can muster.

I understand computers, security, and data. I have made a point to understand the companies that steal your information.

Most are unaware of what is happing with the data being collected. Right now, the rates that you pay for some types of insurance and personal loans are based on what you disclose in social media. It also is based on what you purchase offline and where the transaction takes place. Soon I fear that this same methodology will be instituted in the college admission process along with corporate hiring practices. Thus, it is limiting opportunity and the personal freedoms of expression. Our nation was founded on the idea that we have an inherent right to pursue happiness.

Internet search engines are becoming censored and are no longer neutral in political ideology. Part of the effort behind the personalization movement is being used in a manipulative fashion. Thus, things that are core principles of our Constitution and our way of life are being systematically subverted. It is an inherent danger to our youth who will grow up not expecting that the global communication platform is open to varying ideas.

The internet has challenged the rules and working of many facets of the twentieth century. Newspapers and television have changed the way they do business. The music industry is no longer dominated by labels that were a requirement for an artist to succeed. More books are published every day than ever before and the stranglehold of the publishing industry is becoming increasingly irrelevant.

Imagine an internet experience that belongs to you. It is normal after all; that is the way we experience life. The World Wide Web was created with that and much more in mind. It was a gift that has been co-opted into something that is intrusive, detrimental to the freedom of expression and rapidly becoming the center of manipulation.

We have allowed it to occur; we have fallen victim to own actions of sending, liking, sharing, and retweeting. The systems that we use are being used against us, and it doesn't have to be that way. Sir Tim Berners-Lee who invented the web describes it as a silo effect. Each service on the internet runs in its own space; it is difficult to share things between social networks or other places on the internet. His explanation is from an engineer's service-centric point of view. I am not stating that his point is wrong—far from it. I only suggest that the model of the internet should be human-centric and that machines and the operations of them should be transparent. That is Berners-Lee's point to a degree, although the experience for the user should be equalized across all platforms. Those that join on one platform should be offered automatically on all platforms. Our internet should be a seamless experience not tied to a device or a browser, let alone a service provided.

We are our own silos and what we all want is safety and security within our lives. What has transpired, however, is a system of chaos that was created to invade our personal choices. A system of control and surveillance was adopted to dictate our actions. We are told that it is in the name of commerce and its protections that place each of us and our actions for sale. It comes with a warning, "the internet never forgets." As long as we allow it to be used against us, it will stay a problem.

Those on the internet that create the services we adore are purchasing our data from companies that have stolen our habits using software (spyware) and web bugs. Those are hidden pixels on web pages that track what we do. There are hundreds of spies capturing that data as well, reporting back to companies that hide what they do with the data and sell it all over the internet.

Almost every single news site uses web bugs to track who we are and what we read. It is more than a little disingenuous that we should trust reading something, knowing that we are being spied on. These sites should be transparent in who is tracking us and why. Who is it selling the information to and how is that data being used? This is just the news; there are blogs and social networks, music, sports, games, you name it—every interaction is being collected.

What is done with the data? Is it really just being used for your internal analytics or is there something more? News sites hide what they track about us. It is not just for marketing either. The Soviet secret police did not have as much information about its population as corporate America has right now on the average 9-year-old. There are only a few companies that are misusing the information. The majority of the data collection is benign.

Your child will use the internet in ways that will stretch your imagination. In the coming years, AI (artificial intelligence) and virtual reality will become commonplace in our schools. These will in many ways test the limits in what we believe are the limitations in our own physical existence.

This book was written for caregivers with children of any age. Thus, the intended audience includes parents, schools, youth programs, or anyone seeking to protect children from online exploitation and, very importantly, caregivers who are accountable for the consequences of children's actions online.

The Basics of Online Safety

Perhaps the most basic step in solving the majority of the problems we face is simply talking to one another. An open dialogue is the single most effective approach to understanding and managing the challenges faced by our children. They have much to tell us about the changing worlds they occupy and much to learn from parents who actively participate in their lives and engage with them authentically. Opening and maintaining a dialogue with your children is one of the only ways to understand what they are going through. Psychological research suggests that when younger children want important information, they go to their parents first. This practice will help establish and maintain an open dialogue with older children as well.

It is never too early to begin talking with your children about online matters. Building a foundation of trust and understanding takes time. The goal should be more than just monitoring their online activities, but to promote effective and supportive communication. Our system of corporate manipulation instead encourages each of us to communicate more with faceless strangers than with those next to us. Genuinely supportive communication is not encouraged as it potentially interferes with the intended aims of advertising, sales, and information gathering as described and explored elsewhere in this book.

The online world offers superficial contact that suggests a closeness that is not actually there; rather a virtual connection that is mimicked to trigger a basic human instinct. As described in other chapters, children and younger teens do not have the capacity to understand the social influence the internet commands. While children seek to demonstrate adult behaviors online, they do so without the benefit of an adult's developmental maturity and worldly experience.

From birth, infants observe their parents using all kinds of devices. They might see you use a computer or perhaps if you are like most of America, they note your intense involvement with your cell phone. Even before your child picks up a device for the first time, you should start talking about the nature of your online practices, especially online behavior, safety, and security. It's important that you have this conversation before their innocent peers or online forces can serve as their first contact.

If your children are comfortable talking to you, don't take it for granted that they will bring up security or what some stranger said on the internet. There are many forms of online contact that are not easy to talk about. Some online dangers are difficult to discuss between adults let alone to small children.

The easiest description I can give of the internet is that it is an unfiltered communication platform. The web is just a very small part of the internet. Some of the services we use have web interfaces so it is normal to associate what something is by what you can see. It has connected the world like nothing before it could. It breaks down the barriers of language and social culture. It's far reaching and includes the many that you would not consider, like the warlords and gunrunners, the drug addicts and prostitutes of far-off lands and they all have access to the same systems that you watch cute puppy videos on. You share this space with them, and have the very false belief that they don't affect you if you just ignore their existence.

If you never have experienced a wrong click and ended up on a porn website or a site filled with rantings of someone who is severely mentally ill, you are lucky. These are also on the so-called social networks and are waiting for your child. There is not a magic piece of software or hardware that you can buy to replace true understanding and discussion. What you tell your child, and how you prepare your child for the internet depends on how well you communicate in general. There are filters and programs for sale and subscriptions that will limit conductivity to particular web sites. These have been available since the beginning of the World Wide Web nearly twenty years ago. Some of them work but none of them are substitutes for conversations that you have with your child. The values that you instill will be the foundation by which your child uses his/her decision-making process.

It will be up to you to initiate conversations about the internet. You can use so many situations that are around you in real-world situations. You can also use television but there is a psychological downside to using television as an example for anything. Many of us explain television to small children as make believe. Over time, this gets hardwired and you do not want to mix real life with anything that is on the television. I call it the liar box; its distortion of reality, news, and family life is confusing for plenty of adults, let alone your kids. You should make clear examples in the world so that associative memory can make a real connection.

You should talk to your kids about the other people on its platform, what internet scams and cyberbullying are. If you use social networks, there are plenty of examples of bad behavior. You can use these to talk to your kids. Facebook® and Twitter® are both filled with bad behavior; scams and bullying are commonplace.

If you don't know what to look for, simply search for anything political. You will find every bad behavior on full display.

Over a decade ago, it was popular for people to put computers in their living room so that they could monitor their children's activities on the internet. Today however with our individual devices, cell phones, game systems, and tablets, monitoring children and their activities becomes increasingly difficult. Teenagers often will bury themselves in their room outside your ability to supervise their activities.

It is up to you to create an honest and open environment so that your children can come to you to help guide them. Be supportive and foster an understanding that many of the things that are on the systems are not things that you agree with. Be upfront about your values and how they apply to what you see online. Communicating your values will go a long way in making your children create informed decisions when they face tricky situations.

You should resist the temptation to bring it all up at once. I forget about things from time to time, I get wrapped up in my life too. When you're in a busy family life surrounded by work, school, and evening activities, it becomes difficult to remember that your children need not only reinforcement for themselves but reinforcing ideas, your values about the internet and how we use our devices. It will present itself to your children even if you don't use it yourself.

One thing that you could do is use the calendar application of your choice and put in it reminders for yourself to talk to your children in the future. Just simple reminders can go a long way in having conversations about the unpleasantness contained on the internet.

Like it or not, our connected way of life is here to stay. There are people who make an attempt to hide from it and also there are those that try to embrace every new thing as soon as it comes along.

Honestly I don't know which is more dangerous—the deniers of the new way of life or the crazy people that jump on every new bandwagon. Its absurdity is like a group of clowns directing the bus driving society.

I do know that your children are the focus of a very large group of companies that want to compete with you in shaping your child's ideas on buying the junk that is shoved in front of us all of the time. It should be expressed that it's just for manipulation. It will be up to you how your children handle the tailored manipulative messages.

I do not believe that this system is okay. It is part of the reason that companies are tracking everything that we do in the justification that it's just for marketing. Spying on my every activity to know what my emotional buying points are is intrusive. Websites that cater to small children also collect information about your child and use it.

With children, it's not about making them wiser or giving them some sort of informed experience. It's really about separating your wallet from you. Your children are just emotional toggle switches to most of these companies. It is a vulnerability they can take advantage of. Most of the products shoved in front of you each and every day are overpriced and you do not need them. The companies know that individualized or target marketing is not for you. It is to save millions of dollars to get your child to buy the color blue or pink. It is to convince them that their children should buy those colors too.

When really young children are exposed to the webpages for the first time, you do not want to leave your children alone. The cartoony sites offer lots of games that young children will enjoy. For most of these, what gets left out of most discussions is that the sites are there for what is called brand reinforcement. Television programming or internet programming comes along with commercials for product. Building brand loyalty has been the mainstay of the Disney Corporation for many years. Its products are the various characters that the company creates and promotes. The values that Disney promotes will get instilled into your child. I mentioned them because they are the oldest company that does this; though it is aggressive, it is not the most egregious.

There are other massive companies that openly compete with Disney, with a wide range of characters to push junk and values at your children that, quite truthfully, if you do not pay attention will confuse your child about the values in your own household. This is not an accident; it is a calculated effort made by these companies, some of which are the same ones that are behind big data. These multibillion-dollar companies purposely target children to manipulate you into buying a product.

It is the whole point of their existence to sell you junk that you do not need. Your children are being targeted by these companies to be loyal to a particular brand. You should know this because you've fallen for it over and over in your life and it certainly hasn't gotten you any wiser, prettier, happier, or richer.

By the time your children reach their tween years, data has been collected on them for quite a while. How long they are allowed to be exposed to the systems is just one data point. Their interests have been catalogued for when they turn 13 years old and they become open fodder. They can be directly marketed to because all of the legal restrictions are removed. It was decided that 13 is the magic age by our Congress and it's the Federal Trade Commission that enforces the laws as they are written.

Tweenagers start expanding their own interests and building their own hobbies. It is likely that they will use the internet for additional information for their own interests. It is also the same time that you might want to consider creating time limits on access.

Many parents decide to install internet filters on devices to block unwanted material. It's also about the time that middle school kids learn to defeat the filters. The tech-savviness and curiosity of some young minds will be shaped on a platform that you may not understand. It is imperative that your values be instilled beforehand. What you believe as right and wrong already collides with social forces. We are bombarded with messages that we simply do not agree with. As a result, we pass our values and beliefs over to our children. We do it in the hope that they will depend on them when we are not present.

Keeping track of what your child does online is not hard. Let your child understand what is acceptable, behavior, and you will be monitoring what they do online. Check the browser history then delete it. You will know if they try deleting it themselves from the time stamp. There are videos on Youtube about any subject including how to check your computer for suspicious applications or data files. Make it a rule that walking by and seeing any activity such as closing programs, switching screens, or erratic behavior is ground for terminating the use of the device. Check the machine for file sharing applications. If in doubt what a program is ask your child. Have them explain what the program does. You will know if they are not being truthful.

One of the people I went to high school with went into law enforcement. He was a city cop and over time advanced within his department. I'm sure that he instituted controls on the network and supervised his children very closely. He was shocked to find one day that his daughter's high school had called him because she had been involved in sexting. She had taken pictures of herself partially naked. The pictures had been texted over and over again throughout the school. I found out about this on a social network. All of this really should have never happened. It is wrong at many levels.

While society can armchair every instance in the news about sexting situations, it's just a reinforcing example of the importance of talking with your children about what your home values are.

It is about instilling the values that you have and defining what is acceptable within your home. These things come from what your ideas are. It is not for anyone, including myself, to tell you what the best way to handle this situation may be. It is for you to decide how best to handle these things with your children. Talk to them about the issues, not only what is written here, as there will always be new things. Discuss with your child what your feelings are about in any and all of these situations. As a parent, isolating yourself from society, in my opinion, only ensures that your child will be ill-prepared for the many other influences they encounter in school.

By the time your children reach their teenage years, the internet probably has become more of an annoyance in your life. Beyond values, you need to instill within your teenager the idea of credibility. Fake news is all over the internet. The search engines have violated their terms of trust. Google®, Yahoo®, and Bing® have decided that political and social views are suitable to manipulate. While society clambers to accept personalization for each search, I see it as a mass scale form of censorship. These distortions will cloud real research, driving a conclusion that is predetermined. Artificial intelligence will unquestionably be introduced in searching algorithms in the near future. This will enable searching to be conceptual instead of simply keyword based.

If you want to see a demonstration yourself, pick four news topics at random. These should be things that have no interest to you at all, something completely new to you. The examples I used were "blood diamonds", "Palestine occupation", "Chechen heroes" and "Shania Twain." Depending on what you search for, you will get different result on different devices. Call a friend and ask them to do the same exercise, and compare the results. If you take a picture with your cell as I did, you can see the difference not only in order of appearance but content omissions or placement.

Fake or tailored news is only one consideration. The internet and social networks are littered with people that are not who they say they are. You need to build in suspicion whenever your teen is communicating with someone else. While most people on the internet are not really out to harm anyone, there are bad actors. In the sea of information and ideas, there are sharks that lie in wait. Criminals do place fake profiles on the social networks and they do interact with other people.

My first book was a novel, "Extortionware: A hacker's tale," and was written after I discovered a pedophile and suspected human trafficking ring running on Facebook®. I had turned the information over to the authorities after understanding a little bit of how the operation worked. I did not fully understand what I had discovered at first.

I was approached on another site's chat system and was invited to Facebook® where I chatted with an unknown person for almost a month. The profile picture that was used, I found elsewhere on the internet with an entirely different person. I continued asking questions and giving out as little valid information as I could. Eventually, I discovered that there were over 10 profiles linked to the same profile with hundreds of other men who were supposed friends of all of them.

I normally wouldn't have put such effort into chatting with someone I didn't know, but, I was sick at home with the flu. It really gave me an insight into the lengths to which criminals will go to get money.

I would not expect a teenager to have the life experience to understand that the criminal was just trying to manipulate them. Your teen simply wants to be liked, as does the majority of society that uses the social networks. When we chat with people without video, there is no way to know who that person is. That was one of the founding reasons behind Snapchat being created. It is a video chat system that has its own problems with criminals and porn. Snaps are deleted by its servers after they are opened by the recipient, making it difficult if someone wanted to hide what was being chatted about.

By the time your kid is a teenager, you should be able to anticipate how they will react when they find something online that you would not approve of. Hopefully your teen will have the relationship with you that will allow them to confide that they had found something that was inappropriate. It is an opportunity for you to work with them and to try to prevent it from happening again.

There are all kinds of inappropriate behaviors on the internet. Pornography, violence, and hate speech are all around us. Racism, bigotry, and jealousy permeate society and the social networks. Scattered in the virual world however are identity thieves, hackers, cyberbullies, and predators. Hopefully you have never experienced a predator in your life.

These are disturbed people who do not care who they hurt or how they get what they're looking for. Your children may find a cyber predator disguised as another child. The trusting nature of children is something that predators depend on. It is very important that you know who your children are talking to.

"Approximately ninety percent of all American children between 12 and 17 years old are online and three in four teens access the internet on cell phones, tablets, and other mobile devices. One in five US teenagers who regularly log onto the internet say they have received sexual solicitations via the web." [1]

Internet sexual predators tend to fall between the ages of 18 and 55, although some are younger or older and their targets tend to be between the ages of 11 and 15 years old. In almost all reported cases, all of the victims went voluntarily to meet with predators.

It is very unlikely that your child will be the victim of an online predator. Online predators are all over the internet and actively try to engage with children. We have a tendency to think of ourselves in our own community. Just as we may frequent the same local grocery store, our Facebook® is the people we really know from our own neighborhood. Predators are a global issue that shows itself in communities throughout North and South America as well as in Europe. There is no boundary to the internet and there is no limit to the links by which a predator will react.

While most of the advances happen through internet chat rooms or through instant messaging, they generally begin with sending or requesting sexual photographs. Chat rooms are not only on separate systems, some games and gaming sites also include chat spaces that are filled with pornographic invitations.

Boundaries help children and adults understand and take responsibility for the things that they have control of. The boundaries we draw, privacy among them, begin to define what we believe about our values and our standards. Personal security, if you think about it, is lost with privacy. By forgoing our own boundary of privacy, and allowing our children to believe that it does not exist, can create destructive behaviors within your child. This, I believe, is what causes so many to perceive pornography as acceptable within society.

Major corporations are tracking all of our activities both on the internet and off it as well. Today it is difficult to define offline, since most of us carry personal bugging devices (cell phones) with us everywhere. The electronic systems of payment are tracked as well; card numbers associate who you are to a purchase.

Let your children understand that this is happening too. The majority of society seems oblivious, along with other parents. One potential solution to this is to augment the education and parent-teachers associations. Educators know what is being talked about in classrooms. They may not understand what it is, but these things have names; it should be their responsibility to report them to some formalized structure within the school. While it should not be the school's place to filter or decide what is important, just what is trending, this insight should be shared with parents so they can understand what is being talked about with their child's peers.

This information could then be disseminated to parents to discuss with their children and to research if they so choose. It would empower parents and ultimately allow adjustments to be made in school. The idea that you as a parent can be forewarned of every new technological advancement or societal ill is unlikely without the support of educators.

Monsters On The Net

The internet violates hard-earned lessons from the not-so-distant past. Society was sobered with the realization that predators are in our midst stalking, exploiting, abusing, and even murdering our children. Remarkably, the concept of "stranger danger" and equipping our children to limit access to only designated "safe" adults is quickly being replaced by a culture that weighs everyone's value by their access to as many strangers as possible. Online media teaches our children to seek as many "looks," "likes," and other forms of acknowledgment of their presence online as possible. By default, success on personal media becomes a matter of how many strangers one can attract (a child with 1,000 likes is exposed to strangers, as is a child with 500 or even 50 likes; children simply do not have that many personal, safe contacts). Children use those social networks to provide personal information including text, pictures, and videos across a variety of sites like YouTube, Facebook®, Instagram, Twitter®, and whatever is the currently popular site. Ultimately, this information can be used to exploit/endanger children and/or to make children dupes in identity theft schemes, many of which also impact their parents or the organizations serving children. As a society, we need to resume our role in protecting children and their families from this new form of stranger danger.

If you are concerned about protecting your children online, it will take a lot more than a few simple remedies. A quick search for solutions on Google® or Yahoo® will give instructions to caregivers to merely locate a child's online device(s) in a common place. This step might work for children under 6 years old. However, it won't work with older children and teenagers who can access the internet from any number of devices and locations. Given the acceptance of media in our lives, it can be difficult to accept the need to reconsider how we relate to technology. Caregivers and their children must become informed consumers. Moreover, they must become savvy in how they carry themselves online. While I recommend focusing on legitimate approaches to the problem, it is also necessary to fight fire with fire. For instance, caregivers can instruct their children to practice misdirection of personal information on the internet. They should begin with providing alternative identifying information to satisfy online corporate requirements, which does not provide actual personal information. Your child should adopt a persona that has a first and last name that is not anything like their true one and stay with it. Accompanying information such as the date of birth and email addresses should be used consistently. While it is not my intent to suggest that anyone defraud anyone, spying on your children to sell its actions is far removed from a moral cause.

Know who your friends aren't. It is important to establish with children early on that online contacts that they do not know in person are never really their "friends" and that sites that invite such terms for contacts to help sell their applications do not promote friendship. Ask them to come to you if anyone they do not know asks personal questions, even their full name, birthday, or school level. Security takes diligence and not yielding your principles.

Your children will learn from you and what you do and your actions. You should start as early as you can; let them understand that the internet is a valuable, enjoyable, but dangerous space and that predators take advantage where children get comfortable, especially "new" sites that seem beyond the reach or awareness of grownups.

Some (older) children are sometimes aware when strangers and questionable contacts try to reach out to them online. Adults might be surprised by how often children manage predators on their own. Thus, it is essential for children to trust caregivers. Younger children are vulnerable to thinking that even explicitly inappropriate contacts are the result of their own actions (complicated by their curiosity with elicit sites), which tempts them to conceal those interactions. Caregivers will need to promote a child's trust starting with "no questions asked" rules. For instance, do not provide your actual identity until you prepare for college; that includes any of the growing numbers of online apps that exist on devices.

There are quite a few virtual phone numbers that you can sign up for. A virtual number is a phone number that is forwarded to a real phone number. There are companies that sell virtual numbers all over the internet. You can also get a number from Google®. Just signup for Google Hangouts®; it used to be called Google phone®. The virtual number that you have will be the same number your children use for signing up for internet services. If you do it soon enough, it will become the established number for them. Criminals and professional con players do the same thing anyway. Why should your kid be the target of a cyberbully 5000 miles away? Only the websites really want to know their identity so it can shovel junk at you that you don't need, or worse, track your kid.

If you already have a teen, try to explain why you want them to change all of their social media and email address. If anyone asks, they can respond that they were a victim of identity theft. Over the next several years, it will surpass adult theft which is already at epidemic proportions. Your teenager is vulnerable to not only bad people but from corporate America. One may steal your money, and the other may wreck your life—you pick which is which.

You should be setting up email addresses that are separate for personal, social, and banking. The same should be set up for your children. Make sure the banking email address is never used on the same computer or device that social networks are on. The personal address is used only for the people that we really know, that we have met physically in person. You can use that as a backup address for yourself, and the social address is for junk mail. You know the drill; enter your email address to get access. It's all over the internet; almost every blog, paper, or report wants an address. Fine, here's an address I never look at; you can send your junk there. Show your kids; it will limit the spam that will come that you will need to shift through also.

If you get your kid a cell phone and they have their own number, sign it up using your social media junk mail address. You can always add additional email addresses to any device. Unfortunately, email and text messages are part of our lives. Google®, who attempts to be the daddy of tracking, offers a free phone number through its Hangouts service. I use it when people I don't know want my number. I still get the message, but outside of law enforcement or a hacker with access to Google's ®server, it is virtually impossible for anyone to look up who has the number. If the wrong name is associated with social media, then criminals have one less thing to collect.

There are various dangers that your children will encounter; among them are perverts, trolls, cyberbullies, and confidence games. These exist on almost all chat systems, social media and the internet in general. You want to make sure your children are not embarrassed to tell you when they encounter any of these. You must let them know that there are bad people and on the internet, they can contact you. When your child does encounter someone offensive, block the person and report them. It is really important to remember that the open internet is not for small children and social networks are not for anyone under 13 years of age. The video game consoles that are using the internet are the open internet. Microsoft®, Sony®, and Nintendo® have convinced millions of parents that the game consoles are safe spaces. It is not true, and all of these companies should be ashamed of themselves. Criminals and pedophiles are on the platforms hunting for someone's child.

The social networks make it confusing simply because they offer games that can be played by younger children. Many of the games are geared toward the interests of smaller kids while stating publicly that a child must be 13 to have an account. These companies do not want to deal with COPPA and would prefer to collect information without restriction. That is the age that Congress set to openly market to your children. Facebook®, in particular, has many games that are popular and should not be played on a child's own account unsupervised by someone that is young. An adult should always be present, and I do not mean just in earshot. Young siblings do not have the worldly experience necessary to monitor the internet. The Children's Online Privacy Protection Act (COPPA) imposes requirements on web site and online service operators directed to children under the age of 13 and on operators of other sites and services who knowingly collect personal online information on children under 13 (for further details on COPPA and protecting children online, refer to https://www.consumer.ftc.gov/topics/protecting-kids-online).

Any child who uses the internet on any site that was created for any audience over the age of 13 can be tracked no matter what the age. People often forget that the internet is everywhere all the time. From the brothels of Bangladesh to the war zones in North Africa, to the cartels in South America—it is all the same internet. It is the same one you are attached to on your cell phone, and your child plays on. The only thing separating you and your child from the rest of the planet is the knowledge of who you are.

There is a sea of evil on the net and hackers are the least of a parent's nightmare. There are multitudes of sick people who hunt for images of children, and I'm not referring to Google Images®. Pedophiles call these image depositories bunny spots; they feature pictures of little girls in bathing suits that are shared openly on social networks. Little boys are sought after too. The myth on the internet is that pedophiles are all decrepit old men. However, women have been convicted of the same crimes, though far fewer. Often people who commit crimes are younger; males between 19 and 35 are more likely than any other group to commit a crime, including sex crimes.

Sexual images have been on the internet since long before Tim Berners-Lee invented the web platform. Porn, however, was one of the first types of website to sell services on it. Videos of women and sexual gay images were so prevalent that it spawned two other internet innovations. Applications and appliances were created that blocked whole websites, and pop-up blockers were introduced for web browsers. It was such a problem that Congress passed laws restricting sites that were operating in the United States. As a result, the FBI raided a few of them, and they shut their services down.

While tweens and teenagers may go searching for internet porn, many of the game systems and general chat systems have what I call "the cam girls." These are women and girls who perform sexual acts on their webcams. Most often these are on dating sites, but I have seen them on Facebook® and Twitter®. They will open a chat session and invite the other person to watch them. While younger children are not really the targets of live sexual performers, both male and female older teens will get approached online to chat with one of them.

Many of these accept virtual cash, and for very little money, anyone can chat with a live model that will perform sexual acts from their own bedroom. Some of these are younger women, and some of the sites that promote this activity accept virtual money such as iTunes and Xbox gift cards along with credit cards.

The openness of sexuality on the internet combined with the conservative attitude toward sexuality in the United States has reached many younger children. [2]The act of sending and receiving sexually explicit messages and images is called sexting, and it is not limited to teenagers. It does, however, pose a more serious risk to teens than it does adults.

Teens who engage in the activity may see it as harmless, but many schools and law enforcement agencies see it as child porn when the images are of anyone under the state's legal age of consent. Children have been convicted under the courts and been listed as sexual offenders for forwarding images they have received. While it is not uncommon for courts to rule that records are sealed for juvenile offenders, as mentioned in another chapter, school records do not necessarily follow court orders and the records may be exposed for the rest of the child offender's life.

There is an increasing trend of teen sexting being used in criminal activity. A blackmail technique known as sextortion has been spreading across the internet. The National Center for Exploited Children has recently experienced growth in the number of reports that are being created on its tip line system. There has been an overall increase of self-produced images (sexts) being used to extort underage victims.

"Between 2014 and 2015, there was a 90% increase in the total number of reports; a pattern that has continued, with sextortion reports up 150% within the first several months of 2016 compared to the number of reports in that same timeframe in 2014."[3]

Teens may or may not even know who the blackmailer is. So often, children along with adults start with emotional feelings for people who they really do not know. In the world of the internet, people regularly mix the ideas of the virtual world with the physical one. It becomes very confusing for younger children who are not equipped to comprehend these concepts. Older people really fall for love in the con games that criminals use to bilk them out of money.

Adults also have websites that promote exhibition and visual sexual activity. Teenagers are more likely to fall for criminal activity, as they just want attention and to be liked. In the space of the internet, criminals come from all walks of life, all countries, and both sexes. It is not a stretch to suggest that those who operate pornographic web shows will groom a young person quite easily.

Those who befriend strangers on social networks or while using gaming systems or other spaces online are the most vulnerable. It also contributes if the child openly talks about sexuality or sexual situations. The openness to communication about sexuality can be a sign of approval to a pedophile or a potential blackmailer.

Some blackmailers are known to the victim, while others are people the sender has never met in real life. Often it is someone he or she has befriended on a social network, gaming platform, or other online space. Often the victim is coerced into making a video or simply opens a live video streaming app. Skype and Hangouts are two, but there are many apps that do not require any installation and operate directly by opening a web page.

The blackmailer may threaten to expose the images or video in a public space. There are countless websites that cater to anonymous uploading of pornographic images and videos. They may just threaten to share them with the friends or family of the victim if they do not comply with his or her demands. An analysis was done by the National Center for Missing and Exploited Children; their research revealed that there are three main motives for sextortion:

•To acquire increasingly explicit sexual content (photos or videos) from the child.

•To obtain money or other goods from the child.

•To meet to have sex with the child.

Last year, NCMEC and the Department of Justice released a Public Service video to warn children of the dangers of sharing sexually explicit images online.

With only a few dollars, anyone can locate your child if they use a known email address, like the one you primarily use or the last name that matches yours. A stranger can figure out who a child is on social media by simply looking at the account. Often parents will be listed as someone known or as friends or relatives.

The sites that sell information on the internet include phone numbers and physical addresses along with email addresses. One piece of information along with a full name is enough to find out where anyone lives. Keep in mind that when your children play any sort of game including the game systems, aliases used on those systems are not really any protection from finding someone else's true identity.

Gaming systems in many ways are just like tablets or computers. Most have the ability to browse the internet and/or have chats with strangers. Sexual offenders do use these systems and do ask children sexually charged questions. Their goal is to see if they get a response to their suggestion. It may appear to start as an innocent encounter; these are predators, and your child is the prey. You have no way of knowing unless your child knows to seek you out. You must prepare your child for these encounters before you allow them to use any internet-connected game platform. Let other parents know; it is not something that is generally understood.

"1 in 25 youth in one year received an online sexual solicitation where the solicitor tried to make offline contact. Four percent of the youth in the Youth Internet Safety Survey received solicitations in which the solicitor made or tried to make contact with the youth offline via telephone, offline mail, or in person. These are the online encounters most likely to lead to an offline sex crime."[4]

It is comparatively rare that a complete stranger will send your child a sexually suggestive message. It is far more likely that the message will come from what appears to be a peer. Stranger danger is a problem, but that happens less frequently than a child being assaulted by someone they know and trust.

Chat is built into almost all game platforms, and sexual offenders also play games on the same systems. [5]Back in 2012, 3,500 convicted New York sex offenders were kicked off a few of the major platforms. Companies that participated at the time included Apple, Blizzard Entertainment, Disney, Electronic Arts, Microsoft®, Sony®®, and Warner Brothers®. While the story came out over five years ago, there have been complaints ever since that time. In June of 2017, over 289 arrests were made in Hollywood, California in [6]Operation Broken Heart IV, by the United States Justice Department. Most of the arrests were made for sexual offenders trading in child pornography. [7]One of those arrested was [8]Cushqader Rasul Warren, of Los Angeles. He was arrested by investigators from the Los Angeles Police Department and the Department of Homeland Security.

Warren used the Bandi-Cam program to visually record his computer screen as he played an online computer game named Wizard 101. He would then post these videos on YouTube where he would offer Wizard 101 Game Cards to those who commented on his video. These game cards are needed to enter a paid higher level of play for the game.

Warren would respond to boys who posted a comment and exchange information with them. He then developed an online friendship with them on social media sites. Warren would initiate chat sessions or video calls with the boys, during which he offered the game cards in exchange for sexually explicit videos of the victim.

As of the time of arrest, four victims under the age of 14 were in the United States. Based upon the number of under-aged boys who appeared within Warren's list of Facebook® friends as well as the preliminary search of his computers containing hundreds of thousands of lines of messages and chat logs, this case had the potential to grow to 67 victims. The case was presented to the Los Angeles County District Attorney's Office for consideration with 15 charges being filed.

[9]Social networking sites are websites that encourage people to post profiles of themselves. It is complete with pictures, interests, and even journals. This is done in an attempt to meet like-minded people. Facebook® overuses and stretches the meaning of friendship itself. People who are at best unknown acquaintances are labeled as friends. This is confusing at best to many adults, let alone small children who do not have the ability to understand confusing concepts. Most also offer chat rooms. Most sites are free and some restrict membership by voluntarily asking what age someone is. There are very few if any checks on the internet for how old anyone is.

These sites can be appealing to child sexual predators, too. The sites harbor easy and immediate access to information on potential victims. Even worse, kids want to look cool, so they sometimes post suggestive photos of themselves on the sites.

The problem is very pervasive. Every few months, the media runs stories about the dangers of social networking. Police departments across the nation still receive thousands of complaints per year about children who have been victims of criminal incidents on social networks. These incidents include but are not limited to adults posing as children who convince the child to expose themselves and/or perform sexual acts over a webcam and later extort the child to perform additional acts.

According to an internet safety pamphlet recently published by NCMEC, a survey of 12- to 17-year-olds revealed that 38 percent had posted self-created content such as photos, videos, artwork, or stories. Another survey of 10- to 17-year-olds revealed 46 percent admitted to having given out their personal information to someone they did not know. The likelihood that kids will give out personal information over the internet increases with age, with 56 percent of 16- to 17-year-olds sharing personal information.

Social networking websites often ask users to post a profile with their age, gender, hobbies, and interests. While these profiles help kids connect and share common interests, individuals who want to victimize children can use those online profiles to search for potential victims. Children sometimes compete to see who has the greatest number of contacts and will add new people to their lists even if they do not know them in real life.

Children often don't realize that they cannot "take back" the online text and images they post. They may not know that individuals with access to this information can save and forward these postings to an unlimited number of users. Children also may not realize the potential ramifications of their online activities. They can face the consequences for posting harmful, explicit, dangerous, or demeaning information online, including being humiliated in front of their families and peers, suspended from school, charged criminally, and denied employment or entry into schools.

Posting any comment on social networks or on any forum or chat board can be taken out of context. As an adult, we know this. [10]Children that post comments will find out the hard way what a troll is. Trolls are not cyberbullies; they each have a separate goal. Trolls are visitors who leave inflammatory comments in public comment sections. They may comment on blog posts or online news sites. A troll is looking to grab attention for themselves.

Often they will redirect the other visitor's discussion completely away from the page's topic.

Trolls do this by posting comments that are hateful, racist, sexist, or profane. Trolls might make the content, the author, or the other visitors the target of their incendiary comments. It is the attention that they seek. They attempt to shift attention from the author's content and conversations about the content onto themselves. They want responses to their inflammatory comments from the original author as well as other commenters. The more attention they get in the form of comments directed at them, the happier the troll is. The more attention they get from a website and its readers, the more likely they are to troll that website again.

For trolls, the focus is on being a nuisance to online communities. Cyberbullies target individuals. Rather than posting generally inflammatory statements, they post vicious things about a single person with the goal of disgracing or intimidation. This could take the form of mean-spirited messages, private pictures, or private video concerning the individual the bully is targeting. They could post the information publicly or send it only to their target as a form of taunting.

While trolls try to attract attention for themselves, cyberbullies want to demean and hurt their victims. Trolls are indifferent to the harm their comments may cause. They do not care if their comments cause people emotional distress or not. All they want is a reaction from the community they are trolling. Cyberbullies do not want attention for themselves, but negative attention on their victim. All they want is to cause distress for their victims.

Cyberbullying is bullying that takes place using electronic technology. Electronic technology includes devices and equipment such as cell phones, computers, and tablets as well as communication tools including social media sites, text messages, chat, and websites.

Often children who are targets of cyberbullies are bullied in person as well. Technology, with its integration into society, makes it difficult if not impossible to get away from a bully's behavior. It can happen 24 hours a day, 7 days a week, at any time of day or night and reach your child even when they are alone. The safety of your home can be shattered by a cyberbully.

Those that are victims of such behavior usually do not confide in their parents. They internalize the hurtful messages which can come from anonymous sources, fake social media profiles, untraceable email addresses and text messages that come from fake numbers. On the internet, it is very easy to be a bully to anyone; it is simple to hide and to alter caller ID numbers. It is scary with the knowledge that almost every American citizen's data is sold openly and anyone can be a victim.

Additionally, anyone can be a perpetrator. Even honor students at the top of their class have been caught being a cyberbully.

It is your family, but I believe the problems that will most infect your children come from society. How much of Hollywood's influence will you tolerate in your home? There are general signs your child may exhibit that may indicate something is wrong in their life. If you are close to your children, you will know them. [11] There are other signs that something is wrong in their life including a sudden change in friends, the use of alcohol and/or drugs, skipping school, experiencing in-person bullying, being unwilling to attend school, receiving poor grades, having lower self-esteem, and having more health problems. All of these are signs of problems; there may be more than one present. Either way, there is something wrong. Talk to your child. If you can't get to them, take them to a professional. Be the parent and protect your child.

There are other types of victims as well. The craft is the art of the con; it is all around us, and it is after your children. Both individual criminals and groups that hide themselves as legitimate business attempt to trick, con, and deceive us and our children.

There are cell phone traps, apps that track monthly charges on your bill. There are games that can be installed on just about any device that will trick your child into entering some sort of electronic payment instrument. The initial fee, the price designed to get your approval, is sometimes just a penny. The trick is to get the payment and your card number, which can then be fraudulently charged or just sold to other criminals to use and steal from.

Our government and its law enforcement agencies are overwhelmed with the internet. Most don't even report all of the scams, which is unfortunate.

You can keep your children safe using devices that access the internet. The most important thing you should do is stay involved with what they are doing and monitor their use.

You should discourage your children from using devices outside your presence as long as you can. Don't assume that toys or any device that connects to the internet are in any way safe. Do not trust the intention of any manufacturer to be benign either. The sole reason for creating a product is to sell it, not protecting your child. It is important that your children not disclose any personal information on any website. They should never enter their own name or the name of pets; the internet is not to be trusted with anything. No website is secure. Take it from a hacker—there is no such thing as security on the internet. While I believe that most people are good, there are bad people that will try to contact your child. Make a rule that your child should never meet anyone for the first time from the internet without a parent present. You should know about the meeting ahead of time. If you agree to a meeting between your child and someone they met online, talk to the parents or guardians of the other individual first and accompany your kids to the meeting in a public place.

You should report any loss of any amount of money or any activity targeting your children to your local law enforcement immediately. Do not trust that anyone will follow through; contact the owner of the site and file complaints. Make certain that all privacy and security settings of websites and applications are set not to openly share what your children do in the world. Explain to your children that images, videos, or comments stay on the internet. More often than not, there is no way to take the thing back. You should tell your children to not react and post anything immediately. Trolls and criminals expect an immediate reaction; don't give them control and wait before posting. They should do something else and consider what the outcome will be and then come back to it. Teach your children that they can control cyberbullies and trolls by not reacting.

You should teach your children to not allow strangers to their contact lists. It is not just to protect them; criminals may use them to compromise people they may really know. The internet is never a safe place. Its safety is a myth that was created by large corporations that profit from consumers. Most have been allowed by the government to take advantage of the consumer. You and your children are pawns. Don't allow corporations to spy on your kids. Do not allow your children to use their real names anywhere on the internet. You should take control of their real name. There is a chapter on why later in this book.

Encourage your kids to choose appropriate screen names or nicknames. Do not allow them to use names that would attract a criminal or a pedophile. Taunting these actors can be devastating, and the best thing that you can do is to avoid contact with them. You should monitor who your children are friends with on social networks—what they post and the names that they choose as well. Security for your child is something that you will need to teach your children. It is not just where your children visit.

Show them what a bad site is, show them the dangers, and don't just talk about them. Show them and discuss them. Let them understand that it's not a game. There are bad actors and people who are not nice who play the same game as your child on the same system and will play with them. When your child is young reward them for exposing other acting badly online when they see it. it will help with their development.

Talk to you children about securing their own information and why there are real monsters. Teach them how to create a strong password and not to share it with anyone, besides you of course.

Parents may report inappropriate material and attempts to contact children to the National Center for Missing and Exploited Children (NCMEC). As part of its Congressional authorization, NCMEC has created a unique public and private partnership to build a coordinated, national response to the problem of missing and sexually exploited children, establish a missing children hotline, and serve as the national clearinghouse for information related to these issues. They can be reached 24 hours a day, 7 days week at

1800 THE LOST (1-800-843-5678)
or http://cybertipline.com.

Information can also be reported to
WeTip at 1-800-78 CRIME.

ID Thieves Are After Children

Identity theft is impossible to avoid as long as data brokers sell everyone's information. When credit with a company is established, not all of them check with the credit reporting industry first. As a result, there is not any real fool-proof system that you can use to protect yourself or your children. It is not only when you establish a line of credit either. Medical labs and other companies will routinely send a bill after service is provided. Most often, it will employ the use of a credit collection company on any unpaid debt. Thus, the unpaid amount is entered into the credit reporting system in the name of the individual. There are hundreds of ways to compromise the credit system.

Identity theft can happen to anyone—the very young or the very old. It really doesn't matter if you are wealthy or even if you don't have good credit. It happend to me, and it can happen to you. There are constant reminders in every form of media and there are charlatans in the protection racket. The so-called monitoring services are worthless and the people behind some of the biggest have been likened to professional con-men by the Federal Trade Commission. The credit and banking system has created a mess and ruined countless lives.

There is a myth that gets repeated quite often and is not far from the truth. Identity theft came with the internet. Actually, it came with all of the sites selling our private information that was shortly after 9/11. The United State Government went into overdrive collecting information. What most people do not realize is that private brokerage companies started at the same time buying the same information. Those companies sell the information any way it can, through lists of interest and portfolios.

Everyone is told to check their credit and watch their bank account for unusual activity. If you are like most of us, you take actions to guard your own personal and financial data, but are you protecting your children?

[12]Child identity theft is the fastest growing segment of crime. It affects over five hundred thousand children each year, more than half of them are under the age of six. While other types of identity theft are often reported more vigorously, the theft of children's information is often not reported because the thief is a relative or parent of the victim.

[13]Thieves have targeted children as young as two years old for a wide variety of reasons. Young children typically do not get mail at home and they shouldn't. Sending mail to someone before they can read is a fruitless effort. Besides, what parent would really want to read the advertisements contained in junk mail to their infant? We as a population are so accustomed to junk mail most of us don't read the majority of it anyway. Most often we will just give it a glance and throw it into the recycling system. You should be on the lookout for mail with your child's name on it. It may be the first indicator that something is very wrong. Children that are victims of identity theft can go undiscovered for many years.

Identity theft can be devastating. Worse, most victims are not often believed. Banks and the credit reporting system have a vested interest in collecting bad debt. It becomes worse when you are the fraud victim. After all, you have a state issued identity card, a Social Security Card and you are an adult. Explaining that your child was the victim is difficult at best.

I was a victim myself of a large-scale theft ring that operated in several states. The FBI and local police along with several other state agencies arrested the criminals. Over two hundred of my neighbors were also affected in my town, most on the same street. I know that there are only eight companies that have all of the information that would be needed to commit the crime by the criminals. I have a suspicion which company did it. I do not, however, have any proof and have chosen to attempt to change the system. I have a petition online with the full story about the event. You can find it through this URL: https://www.change.org/p/fix-our-credit-system

As a parent or guardian, you will need to protect your child. The first thing you should do is issue a freeze with Chex Systems. Often banks query this company before instituting a new account for new customers. It may stop the junkie or hardened meth head from using your child's identification to establish an account. But some criminals will bypass this system also. The banking industry is full of holes. If a kind-looking grandmother, who has fifty thousand dollars in an account, asks the branch manager to create a new account, they will. They will open an account for distant nieces and nephews also. There is no law (thankfully) that Chex Systems needs to be consulted on every transaction. There is only hindsight to rely on, truths that are hidden from the general public about the industry. It has forced us to trade security for convenience and shifted responsibility to people without providing enough information to create an informed decision. The banking industry is corrupt and abusive in my option because regulation allows it to be.

Chex Systems is the bank fee enforcement system. People are reported to Chex Systems for not paying bounce fees or for bank service charges. The banks use Chex Systems to block someone who cannot afford to pay all the fees from establishing another account at an alternative institution. There are millions of people that cannot get a traditional bank account. Since many of them are poor, they may not realize that there are banks all over the internet that do not do business with Chex Systems.

Most of the online banks require basic information, photocopies or cell phone pictures of documents, like a driver's license and Social Security Card. Apparently, no one heard of Photoshop, or they don't really care. I believe that the banking industry does not care about security. It has shifted the responsibility of account integrity to the consumer. It only wants the appearance of security so it can overcharge for its services. It is not a coincidence that fees were raised in the banking industry, only after we moved from a paper system to an all-electronic one.

A freeze in Chex Systems is free as opposed to the other traditional credit reporting companies. It is better than no protection. In a way, the security in the banking system is like using a torn condom; it is just the timing that counts.

https://www.chexsystems.com

You should order a freeze with Chex Systems with all of your children. It may stop someone from opening most bank accounts in your child's name. You can also unfreeze the account anytime you want. However, there may be a delay of a day or two when the system updates at the bank you want to use.

Many people without money believe that no crook would want their information. Recently a company I do work with was a victim of a phishing scam. An email was sent to the accounting office to send a transfer of money to an account number. The money was not sent, and the police were notified. The scammers used a checking account number belonging to a 12-year-old in a nearby city. The police would not disclose any other information about the incident, but it is a prime example of the problem that your child could face.

You may think that the companies you know for credit reporting would have it as its core business. Actually, the credit reporting aspect is a small part of its services. Most make money from a wide range of services, including criminal background checks , pre-employment, landlord tenant pre verifcation and what is called the list business. The list business is selling your name, home address and phone number to anyone based on a category that the company assigns you to. When your child signs up for baseball or soccer and you buy equipment, both your child and you personally are put on a list for sale with others in that activity. Provided are links to each of the three major credit reporting companies marketing list pages.

https://www.transunion.com/direct/servicesolutions/
marketingservices.page
http://www.equifax.com/compiled-data/
http://www.experian.com/small-business/mailing-lists.jsp

There are hundreds of companies that want to market junk to you and your child. How you or your child gets on a list vary. It can be as simple as clicking on the wrong link or entering a contest. It could be purchasing a specialty item at a boutique. I am currently experiencing the ugly shirt syndrome: I clicked on a very ugly shirt to look at the pattern, now everything I look at, at home or on my phone, has display ads with the same ugly shirt.

Your children's interests will be traced as well, including from the Disneyesque or its competitors, through pop artists and clothing styles. The thing that you must remember is that it is for sale, anything that is collected no matter how benign or insignificant it is. It all is sellable data to the system. It is collected to trick you and manipulate your children into confusing what is needed or wanted.

Employee and tenant background checks are also offered from the data these firms have collected. Some of these feed the information on sites that sell information about anyone. The web server simply talks to the server at the reporting companies for address information, name, etc. These are also connected to what is called big data to verify your address, phone number, or any other thing about you like your favorite color or the car you had when you first started driving.

All three of them use credit reporting to shield the activities under regulation. TransUnion and Experian both sell things that truthfully are off topic and disturbing. All three of the companies also charge for freezing your credit report or protecting your child's report. It is just another profit center that the industry created after institutionalizing instability in the credit system. There is a charge because individual state legislators have been lobbied and wrote that into law, and each state charges a different amount. This was done to guarantee that the federal system would never write a regulation that would make the freeze totally free. The companies use identity theft as another way to create a profit.

Most people do not understand that state law supersedes practically all federal regulation. When I was in school many years ago, I was taught the popular myth, when in fact it works the other way around. Out of the 50 states, it is just an example of the power of the consorted industry to have 49 individual state laws written and adopted into law. The price that you would have to pay to freeze your child's credit was set by your state. The price for ordering a credit freeze varies, and in some states, there is no charge.

You should really check your child's report. When accessing your child's report for the first time, you may have some difficulty.

The companies will represent that they are protecting the data; these are very large organizations and the first phone call you make may be answered in the Philippines or India.

If you do call overseas, most telecentres have a two or three then back to the US rule. It's not a published rule; you won't find it written anywhere. It was discovery made some years ago when technology support got shipped overseas. When you want to talk to someone in the United States you have to talk to two or three overseas support people before you are "allowed" to talk to someone state side.

When ever you do have to call remember to not get frustrated and hang up. The call center was placed there to frustrate you into giving up. Just start with the first person and ask your question; you may need to rephrase your request to the operator. If the person on the phone does not have a good answer or understand what you want, ask for the supervisor. You may need to demand to be connected to the supervisor. This may have to be repeated; if you still do not have an answer, demand that you be connected to the United States. The hold time varies but count on a phone call lasting an hour or more.

You should start your requests at Experian. In 2013, it became the verifier for the Social Security Administration website online. It has direct access to all Social Security Numbers, names and dates of birth. You should check that you have access and to your children's credit report and to the Social Security Administration immediately instead of when you need something. Otherwise, you will be forced to visit one of the Social Security administrations offices to straighten out your access when you really need it. All data brokers have inaccurate data about all of us. Experian is by definition a broker that is also regulated and is known for its own issues with inaccurate data. You can find many people all over the internet that have had troubles.

[14]In 2003 an amendment was added to the Fair Credit Reporting Act (FCRA) after which a requirement was made that credit reporting agencies provide, upon request, a free credit report every twelve months to every consumer. The goal was to allow consumers a way to ensure their credit information is correct and to guard against identity theft.

[15]A joint venture was created by the biggest three credit reporting agencies, Equifax, Experian, and TransUnion. Central Source LLC was created to oversee their compliance with FACTA Central Source, then a toll-free telephone number, a mailing address and a central website, AnnualCreditReport.com, were set up to process consumer requests.

While the typical misleading banner of the website displays "AnnualCreditReport.com the only source for your free credit reports authorized by federal law," you can get a copy of your report directly from the companies. There are two other reporting companies that the website does not check either, Innovis and PRBC.

If you have never heard of the last two, you're not alone, and it should stand as a reminder that there are other companies that have information about you that sell it and fall outside of FACTA. Your pseudo-score that is sold by various companies and the so-called criminal background checks are not accurate at all. I wrote at length about that issue in my book A Right to Property.

You probably won't want to go through the hassle of checking all five bureaus annually for a child under 8 years old. But starting at 12 years old, you should make it a habit and teach them how to do it themselves and to be secure. If your child has been a victim, there will be enough time before they turn 18 and need the credit for college. You may not become aware until your child is turned down for a job or loan due to a horrible credit history. Most things are removed after seven years. However, collection companies will sell bad debt and restart the clock over and over. Even though your child was innocent, the credit reporting companies will turn a blind eye to you if you discover it more than three months after the occurrence.

To order a credit freeze or to contact each of the companies individually for your reports, you can use the addresses below. The links to the internet will work as well. Just be aware that searching on the internet may yield fraudulent sites that are designed to steal your information.

Equifax
P.O. Box 105788
Atlanta, GA 30340
1-888-298-0045
Equifax Security Freeze
https://www.freeze.equifax.com
Equifax Regular site
https://www.equifax.com/

Experian
P.O. Box 9554
Allen, TX. 75013
1-888-397-3742.
https://www.experian.com/freeze/center.html

TransUnion
P.O. Box 6790
Fullerton, CA. 92834
1-888-909-8872
http://www.transunion.com/

PRBC
1640 Airport Road, Suite 115
Kennesaw, GA 30144

https://www.prbc.com

Inovis
PO Box 1640
Pittsburgh, PA 15230-1640
https://www.innovis.com/

Under the regulation, anyone who has a credit terminal can order a full report. There is also what is called header reports that are sold. Back in 1997, headers were a hot topic that garnered media attention which in turn caused additional regulation aimed at protecting consumers. What was being sold at the time was all of the private information in your report: date of birth, Social Security Number, and current and previous addresses with your name. It is the same things that brokers now sell openly on the internet without your Social Security Number. It only goes to prove that brokers are the real cause of the rise of identity theft.

One seller of your child's personal information is Exact Data in Chicago. It is one of the most egregious of sellers. The information about consumers comes exclusively from the Acxiom Corporation®. Exact Data is the seller, but Acxiom® is the cultivator of the information about you and your family.

You will need to be vigilant in demanding that your children's information is removed from data brokers. The companies have no real right to any of the information, but they will insist that they do. Tell Acxiom® no more. Demand that they purge your data from its computers and the data on your children; it is all your property. There is no excuse for your data to be in the hands of anyone else.

Use this link to opt out of Acxiom® for you and your children
https://isapps.acxiom.com/optout/optout.aspx
You should also send them a letter
if you need a template visit
https://www.itsmyinfo.org/cease-and-desist/

Acxiom Corporation
601 E. Third Street
PO Box 8190
Little Rock AR 72203-8190

If you would like help in contacting brokers and mailing letters, you can visit my website. You are welcome to contact me. If you use social media let me know you are out there. I have a privacy kit available for this company and many others. Tripelix.com

You should stay alert for the sign that your child's identity has been compromised. There are things that you can look for that may seem out of place.

- The IRS sends a notice that your child owes taxes or was claimed as a dependent on someone else's return
- Your child has been denied a driver's license or a bank account
- You receive credit collection calls or bills that are addressed to you child
- You receive credit card or loans offers in the mail addressed to your child
- You receive mail from anyone to your child for any reason.

The mailing list industry does sell children's information. While there are many mailing list companies, not that many sell children's information.

I have a website that has updated information about other companies that you should remove your children's information from. Additionally, stay cautious about releasing sensitive information. Learn the NO word. People often ask for information that they really do not need because it is on a form.

As a parent, the best thing you can do to protect your child is to be careful when divulging your child's information. Our Social Security Number system has real problems, and you really should never give out your child's number. The full number has three parts, and the last four digits are the most important. The first three numbers are the state of issue; the next two are a group code for the year of issue in the state of issue.

Shred all documents, even school records and seemingly benign information with your child's name on it. Thieves can use that data to gain access to more information. Most communities have recycling programs that employ people that will work cheap inside of them. These are the people that see all of the things that come through.

Never throw out your name on junk mail—shred, shred, shred.

Make sure that any activity your child participates in uses the information properly and handles it with care. If a sports team requires a birth certificate for sign up, ask how the information is stored and what safeguards are in place during storage.

Teach your children to keep personal information private when they are online. Social networking sites can be a goldmine for identity thieves.

If you discover your child has been a victim of identity theft, file a police report and get a copy of the report. Contact each of the five credit reporting bureaus to notify them of the fraud, and follow their advice for next steps.

Scamming Children For Profit

The internet is filled with scams and scam artists. Most people falsely believe that the majority of scams come from faraway places, like Nigeria. The truth is that the majority of scams come from the United States. The meth epidemic and other drug dependencies may have a lot to do with it.

Most of the scams are targeted at the elderly. However, there is an increased effort at scamming young people. The overall naiveté of youth makes them an easy target for a wide variety of thieves. Adolescents don't even realize they're handing over personal information that can be used for identity theft or your financial loss. More often than not, the scams will start online through the use of email or pop-up windows that ask for verification of sensitive information.

There have been several reports of instances of malware running on Mac and Windows PCs that create a pop-up window. The windows will ask for a Social Security Number, date of birth, or other sensitive information. The malware will then send that information back to the criminal.

[16]Recently the concentration of scams targeting young people has been done through Snapchat, text message, and emails. There have

been scams on Snapchat in which the victim receives a message that they have won a prize and they are instructed to click on a link which installs malware on the device. There have been scams targeting young girls in the UK claiming to be from a legitimate modeling agency. The scammer will trick the girls to send them head and body shots. After the real modeling agency had multiple requests on its Facebook® page, ACA modeling wrote:

" We do not send out requests for people to join on any social media platform."

Young girls who have shown an interest in modeling have been targeted in an email scam. The reason that children are bombarded with email offers and spam comes from a common myth. They gave their email address to the scammer. Scam operators can buy your teenager's email address from data brokers.

There are two lists that include girls that are for sale by Exact Data in Chicago. It sources the information on consumers from the Acxiom Corporation®. Any pedophile, rapist, or criminal can simply buy the list of girls with blond hair and blue-eyed girls or brown eyes and black hair that are all under 14 years old and live with a single parent who rents.

The industry calls these details selects out of its mass database of everything your child does.

"The Hip Fashion—Trendy Teens mailing list provides accurate, highly deliverable consumer information for your next email marketing, telemarketing, or direct mail campaign. The consumer records in this list are consistently updated on a monthly basis through National Change of Address processing as a service to our customers. Containing name, postal, email, phone, and other demographic information, this mailing list of Hip Fashion—Trendy Teens allows businesses to build relationships with their niche target market.

Postal Records (Universe) 13,780,714
Email Records 1,244,479
Phone Records 873,697
Social Media 6,835,234

The Fashionable Youngsters—Tween Apparel Buyers mailing list presents extensive, up-to-date consumer contacts for your next email marketing, telemarketing, or direct mail campaign. The records in this are continuously qualified through a strict maintenance process in order to provide data of unmatched excellence. Including (but not limited to) consumer demographic information, this specific mailing list of Fashionable Youngsters—Tween Apparel Buyers enables decision-makers to build new long-term customer relationships.

Postal Records (Universe) 2,069,281
Email Records 181,244
Phone Records 123,399
Social Media 1,026,363

Each of the numbers represents the number of teenagers or tweenagers in the list. Brokers do not generally care where the information comes from. The people on the list came from some source or a group of sources. It could also come from something that was purchased by a parent or by a television program that was watched. It could also be from browsing the internet while logged into a social media account. There are various ways that people end up in general interest lists.

In June of 2017, a girl who was under 18 years old was contacted to participate in a modeling opportunity. The request came from a supposed relative of someone known to the victim, who was seeking a model for a clothing project that they were working on.

The teen was then sent to a website application that would supposedly measure the girl's body. [17]The girl posed in front of a webcam in various poses, in different stages of undress. The girls are falsely told that their interaction with the computer program is private and their actions are not visible to others, according to the police investigating the incident in what appears to be an elaborate form of voyeurism.

On July 7, 2017, The Newtown Connecticut police department was contacted by the National Center for Missing & Exploited Children. The complaint that was taken in by the center was that a resident under 18 years old had been contacted and was directed to a web-based measuring application.

There are real applications that do use the camera on cell phones and computers to measure clothing for tailors. Some of these claim that the applications are 20% more accurate than having to measure by hand. These applications make it so anyone can purchase custom-fit clothing from an online retailer.

Many teenagers want to be trendy and have all of the latest designer styles. The knockoff business runs throughout the world. For many years the customs enforcement within countries made it difficult for brand-name fakes to be imported. The internet has changed that so anyone can sell and ship anything throughout the world. The legitimate marketplaces are overrun by fake and knockoff designer brands. Over the last few years, some of the name brand designers have made an effort in proactively pursuing sites that sell fake merchandise.

This hasn't stopped the sale of forged goods, far from it. Good forgeries are still sold in the open. Bad copies, however, can end up on designer bargain sites. Some of these operate in the open, stating that they are selling copies and some misrepresent the brand entirely.

[18]You may have seen online advertisements yourself for cheap iPhones, electronic gadgets, designer clothes, handbags and other luxury goods

being sold at just a fraction of the retail price. There is a television advertising campaign that operates an online scam of sorts. What looks like an auction is not one. Your children may fall for it; you must tell them about scams and call them out for what they are. It is foolish to assume that just because it comes from a trusted source it is legitimate. The search engines for example have sold criminals display ads that contained viruses. Online news sites have sold banner advertising and so has Facebook® and every other social network.

Many of the online advertisements are scams aimed at unsuspecting individuals who are looking for a great deal. However, these scams don't only exist online. Your teen can be approached anywhere with offers that are too good to be true. Unfortunately, in most cases, the goods do not exist. Your teen will hand over the money to a scam artist, and they will never see the promised merchandise. A talented scam artist will make your child somehow believe that they are responsible for the loss. They will perhaps convince them to be embarrassed. If done correctly, your child may never tell you about the incident. The embarrassment is what the scammer counts on, so you won't go to the authorities. Most of these scams are unreported.

A man contacted the police to report that his 13-year-old son was the victim of an internet fraud. The man went on to explain that his son was involved in trading sneakers on the internet. The teen had recently sent a pair of Nike Champion sneakers valued at $1,000 to an individual who had agreed to exchange them for a different pair of Nikes, but when the package arrived, it contained a pair of old sneakers instead. When the victim attempted to contact the sender, the phone previously used had been disconnected.

It comes down to understanding how much something is. If it is priced considerably less online, you might want to ask why. In China name brand electronics retail for more money than they do in the United States. People in China pay more for electronics from the US because the items don't break. The same holds true for clothing. Real name brand clothing wears differently. I happen to like well-made men's clothing. I can say from experience that the mass-produced over-priced junk sold in many stores does not look as nice or last as long as the garments that are well made that are bought from stores that do not occupy shopping malls.

On May 18, 2014, DaphneDresses issued the following press release: [19]"China-based Fraudulent Prom Dress Websites Continue to Scam American Teenage Girls According to DaphneDresses. com

"Daphne Dresses, a leading online retailer of authentic prom dresses, has found that the trend of China-based websites marketing and selling knockoff designer dresses to unsuspecting American consumers continues to grow this prom season. These websites have a devastating impact on the prom industry, as last year alone, American prom dress designers and prom retailers (both online and offline) lost more than $100 million in retail sales to rogue China-based websites.

"These websites use Google adwords® to advertise, as well as the original designer's images and trademarks, to sell poorly made knockoffs to teenage girls and their parents who believe they are getting a deal on their designer prom dress," says Jon Liney, co-founder of DaphneDresses.com.

"The knockoff dresses do not fit properly and are poorly made, look nothing like the real designer dress, and can take months to ship. Even worse, consumers risk having their credit card information stolen.

"Thousands of American teenage girls and their parents are left scrambling as their big night approaches to find a dress in replacement of the one that either never showed, or wasn't at all what they expected," continues Liney. "By that point, the season's hottest dresses will have been long-gone, and the selection that's left may be rather disappointing for the girl who had her heart set on her dream dress."

While industry-wide efforts have closed thousands of these sites, new fraudulent sites show up each day in internet search results, boosting company legitimacy through fake product reviews and discounts.

Daphne Dresses has a guide to help consumers identify a fraudulent dress website and know how to purchase an authentic prom dress: http://www.daphnedresses. com/buy-authentic-prom-dresses-online/."

You should tell your children about the brand names you buy and why you buy them. There are deals and bargains, but you should be consulted when buying products off of the internet. Often we as parents forget that our children don't understand why we do many things. We take it for granted that they know things that have never been discussed and it can be a cause for peril.

There are many scams that will result in the computer, cell phone, or device being infected with a virus. These applications are targeted at children to take over the device and steal the information, like contact data. Criminals use this information, and data brokers buy this information and use it to sell other products and again to sell to criminals. [20]Children should be told that "Free" music downloads and ringtones apps for cell phones are not really free. Some of these will only work for a short time then require payment. Some companies target teens for these "free" services that send new ringtones and images on a regular basis. However, what they don't advertise is that this service comes with a hefty fee that'll be added to the phone bill each month. Many of these fees appear on the phone bill with vague terms that aren't easily understood by consumers, making it difficult for parents to realize what they're paying for.

Whenever you make a payment on the internet, be careful with your credit card. The credit system is not safe, and you hear about cards being compromised all of the time. You can protect your money and your children by limiting how much money can be stolen. Use gift cards that you can buy at most major drug stores. Visa, MasterCard, and American Express all have them, and for a few dollars you can buy a card and put money on it to use with what I call risky services. The services that perform legitimate transactions usually will offer alternate ways of paying including PayPal. It should be a big red flag to you when a site only takes payment via credit card. While there are some protections from using third-party paysites, having control of the purchase is a better way to go.

There are many legitimate sites and services that market music. Pandora, Amazon, iTunes, and YouTube all offer music streaming and some downloading. If your child really likes an artist try to purchase tracks directly from the site of the artist.

There are free things at the recycling center and occasionally on Craigslist. Not much is really free on the internet. Many of these services for games and music are set up to steal credit card information or to spy on the person using the application. Data brokers are not the only group to worry about on the internet. Foreign governments also want to know who your child is, who they are close to, and who their friends are. The reasons behind foreign governments spying on American children are varied and are beyond of the scope of this book. You should just be aware it happens and try to avoid it whenever possible.

The data brokers are behind many of the sites on the internet. The industry claimed to be worth over 400 billion dollars in 2016. It attempts to collect every facet of your child's life any way it can. Lotteries and contests on the internet are run by some of the seedier actors, just asking for an email address and giving nothing in return.

There are occasional contests on sites that are legitimate, and I played and won things. Some of those are operated by tech magazines and by the Hollywood studios for free movie tickets. I see contests all the time on the internet on other sites and ignore them.

There are scammers that run fake contests in the form of literature, poems or artwork. Most often these are not really contests but require money to publish a book that the scammer sends back to you. These are all more expensive than creating your own book. The price of publishing has changed dramatically. Even a series of short stories can be made into a professional book for very little money. Bookbaby, CreateSpace, and Smashwords will publish any book and put it on Amazon for very little money and even sell you a printed copy. The cost for your own book is far cheaper than the entry fees charged.

There are so many more scams it would occupy a book in itself. You should teach your children that the internet is not safe. All devices that connect via Wi-Fi can be potential hazards and do not trust that people you know are who they say they are on the net. You should teach your child to recognize scams. The innocence of childhood can expose an entire household's devices to viruses and family members to online predators, scams, and identity theft.

While the internet can be the source of many scams, it also provides information to help you fight those scams. In fact, there are online sources dedicated to keeping you and your children aware of online threats and internet scams.

Following is a short list of sites that you can visit for more information.

The National Center for Missing & Exploited Children
www.missingkids.com/

National Cyber Security Alliance | StaySafeOnline.org
https://staysafeonline.org/

Scambusters.org
Internet Scams, Identity Theft, and Urban Legends

https://www.scambusters.org

Safe Kids Worldwide
https://www.safekids.org/

The internet is the most deceitful medium humans have ever created that is connecting humanity and hope like nothing before it could.

The Limitations
Of Monitors

Throughout this book, it has been expressed that applications that block access or track the things your child does simply are a bad idea. Many of us turn to electronics or quick fixes to solve complicated problems. For some problems, there is not a quick fix. There are professionals who can help your child and help you understand why your child is doing what they are doing.

If your child is drinking alcohol and using drugs, there are things you can do about it. You see, I was one of those children. I have seen some of my peers end up with a lifetime of problems. Many of my childhood friends ended up with the American dream. I am not exceptional, and I don't believe that I am special. Strange luck has no real explanation.

Find something—anything—that your child has an interest in, and guide them into the activity. Video games are not what I mean. Video games are isolating. So much of our society is geared toward not communicating with anyone else around you. It really is counter to the entire human existence.

Find an activity that forces them to meet new people. Change their surroundings by enforcing the new activity. Music, art, or dance classes can sidetrack your child. Martial arts also has its own philosophy and is engaging. There are activities that foster participation at all age levels. Most of all, you should be supportive. There is no rule written that they can only be in one activity either—whatever gets your child away from the person or people supporting the disruptive behavior.

One Sunday night, a mother opens the door to her 16-year-old daughter's bedroom to find she is not there. The front door was closed and not locked. The police were called, and her diary she left behind gave the family clues. She had been chatting with people online and developed an online romance with a 32-year-old man who convinced her to run away with him. Actually, she had encountered a predator, a person who looks for victims. They carried on an online chat through the various systems. Her parents took away her cell phone and limited her time on the computer at home. Predators are a different type of person than someone who is a pedophile. It is an over-used word on television and in society in general. Predators hunt for victims and will say and do anything in order to dominate their prey.

So she used her friend's devices and the computer from school. Her new friend was always there to support her against her evil parents. She had written in her diary that she should not listen to her parents. This was stated by her father, in a televised newscast, four days later. His eyes red from tears, he pleaded for the safe return of his daughter.

[21]"He gradually wormed his way into her good graces, he coerced her into listening to him and not following our directions, and the next thing I knew my daughter wasn't communicating with me," he said.

Burns said Hailey has Asperger's Syndrome, and he admits they've had behavioral issues with her before. But he said his family did everything to make sure this wouldn't happen—but it did.

"We had tried to eliminate all social media from our home. Telephones, computers... and she still found ways around it. She would use friends' smartphones or the school library computer," Burns said. "If you're not vigilant, you're going to wake up one day, and your child is going to be gone, and you're going to be sitting here on a camera pleading with them to contact you," Burns said.

The neighborhood had posters of Hailey, and so did missing children websites. The FBI worked the case to no avail. She was missing, and as time slowly rolled by, the posters came down too. Hailey was still not found for a year.

[22]Michael Wysolovski confined Hailey Burns in an upstairs bedroom of his Duluth, Georgia home, telling her she'd be arrested if she left. He reportedly controlled every aspect of his captive's life by keeping a food journal detailing how many calories she had eaten each day.

The neighbors reportedly had seen the teen unloading groceries from the car. They thought they were just a quiet couple. She had waved to one of them once. "They just kept to themselves," another one remarked.

An American student studying abroad in Romania was chatting one day on Facebook® and started a conversation with someone she believed was in trouble. The person typed that she was being held captive but did not know where she was. The student convinced her to take a picture out the window. She then told the student her name and that her parents were looking for her. The student then reached out to Hailey's parents who contacted the police.

Hours later, Hailey was rescued. After a year missing with no contact, it is rare that the child ever is recovered. The majority of unsolved runaway cases are solved by someone finding a decomposed body. In Hailey's case, there was no filter that could have stopped her from communicating with the monster that she found. If she had a cell phone, it might have added clues to her whereabouts sooner perhaps. Standard SMS messages are stored at cellular carriers. While consumers can often not get ahold of that information, the carriers have built a profit center of selling information to police departments.

There are applications that do track the whereabouts of your child. While I don't believe in filters at home, you should know who your child is communicating with. Filters are painful and have many false positives. Local ones that go on the computer often will make the computer slower and interfere with using it. Since many use the Xbox and other devices that carry the ability to chat and view the web, limiting one device over the other is self-defeating, especially if you are paying for a piece of software. It is systems that have chat services enabled and other things outside the computer filter. It can be powerful. Just remember that if your child knows that they are being watched and monitored, they will do things to bypass the tracking.

Putting a filter on your home computer that constantly interrupts its use will entice the user (your child) to use someone else's computer or device. The other consideration is that there are many different applications that work on phones, computers, and tablets. There are only a few that truly have cross-platform compatibility. K9 security is one such application. It is a filter with the ability to block access to websites in more than 70 different categories. It is backed by some of the largest internet protection companies including Symantec and Norton. It allows you to override access to the sites with a password. While it does protect the computer and phone from most tampering, be aware that having administrative rights to any device can override your protective efforts.

You should not give your child the administrative password to the computer anyway. Most often people will use computers and other devices with administrative rights. In the Windows environment, this has been a long-standing problem for computers that were not part of a domain. Generally speaking, that is a computer operating system used in an office environment. An example of this is the Windows 7 or 10 operating system. Mac-based computers also have the same fundamental issue. You should create a new user for each of your children with unique passwords that are separate from you own access. You should assign no rights to install or change the computer to your child.

The computer will prompt the user any time software is added. This also will ensure that applications that are installed like K9 security are more difficult to tamper with. If your child simply searches for remove, disable or bypass K9 or any other filtering application, they will find a wide range of YouTube videos. Most of these attacks target older hardware flaws with Windows and Mac operating systems.

Older hardware is dependent on what is called the bios of the computer. When you turn a device on, you will see a short splash screen that may say something like a manufacturer name or symbol. This is the program that loads first before the rest of the operating system loads. In Windows-based computers, often this program can have password protection added to it. The newer generation of machines has introduced a secure boot mechanism within the bios. Macs, as of this writing, have not employed the enhanced boot security at startup.

The danger with all of these devices is simple: your child can simply download a bootable CD-ROM or USB stick image and use that. Using these boot methods will bypass any so-called protection that you have placed. This again is the base of the problem; you need to communicate with your child. Instill your values in your child. Let them understand why you are against pornography, gambling, drugs, and alcohol use. Discuss these things with them and make an impact with them. If, however, you are having the discussion while inhaling a Marlboro cigarette, while you have a beer open and are playing scratch-off tickets, it is doubtful that your child will hear your suggestions.

Knowing where your child is all the time is easier with the personal bugging devices that we carry. The major carriers and a host of other apps will allow a parent to know where their child presumably is. [23]Be aware that there are apps that can fake the position of a GPS. I use one on Android called fake GPS. Your child could use it and fool the phone into being at a friend's and actually physically be miles away. Nothing truly beats calling in when staying over so you can ask for the other parents, just to make sure when in doubt.

While the app market is flooded with applications that can track GPS information, there is one application that stands out for tracking and notifying parents of potential problems. Some parents feel that the internet is somehow like a diary. There are predators on the internet. Some have disguised themselves as school children, to fool you and your child. Always ask, "How do you know this person?"

Dig deeper if the first answer was not clear.

Some parents do not understand the dangers of the internet. It is sold to be safe by the banking industry, which gets hacked all the time. It is sold as a kid's toy by internet service providers, and it is neither safe nor is it a toy.

If your child has problems doing things with technology that they shouldn't, then you have a bigger problem than monitoring will solve. Just as in Hailey's case, the parents removed what created an evidence or clue trail. Most filters no longer work anyway. Not so long ago, the web wasn't encrypted. Web traffic on most social networks is now in https sessions. What was going on was traffic on the internet was being captured by third parties. When you logged into a social media site, the information could be seen by anyone watching the wire between the computer and the website. I'll stick to computers for now, but all devices work similarly. If you were on an open Wi-Fi connection, your login information, meaning your email address and password, were exposed to anyone else watching. When you use an encrypted method like https, the traffic is encrypted until it reaches the server. No one on the outside can read what is being sent, in theory. There are ways around that, and I will not get into them here.

This is the problem with filtering; almost all websites use https encryption. The social networks, the search engines, and even the porn sites for the most part use encryption. Most of them use it to protect the login information. It also was implemented to keep the traffic to itself. This means that an external filter cannot read the traffic; it cannot read cuss words in chat messages or see the file names on pornographic sites or read the contents of emails.

All that is left is URL filtering. That is knowing the name of every good and bad website and blocking or allowing the entire site. Again, this poses a problem since people cuss on Facebook®, idiots post pornography on Twitter®, and there are full-length pornographic movies on YouTube.

Not being able to read the contents of chat messages is a problem for any sort of strategy based on snooping on a device. It is also one of the reasons that Snapchat is so popular. The messages cannot be read by anyone except the recipient, and the message is deleted after it is read.

Not one of the cell phone apps that allow monitoring of email, SMS text messages, or most other instant messaging application can read Snapchat.

[24]Snapchat is a mobile app and service for sharing photos, videos, and messages with other people. Once you view a message received via Snapchat, it is automatically deleted. This makes the service ideal for sharing quick updates with friends without accumulating media or messages on your mobile device.

The Snapchat app is available for iOS and Android devices. Once you download and install the app, you can create an account and add friends. You can then take a "snap" and send it to one or more of the people in your friend's list. You can also use Snapchat to send quick text messages that disappear once the recipient reads them.

To take a photo in Snapchat, simply tap the capture button while the camera is active. To take a video, hold down the button for a few seconds to record a short clip. Once you've captured your photo or video, you can swipe right or left to apply filters or add other effects. You can tap the "T" icon in the upper right to add text and tap the pencil icon to select a color and draw on your snap before sending it. If you're taking a selfie, you can press and hold on your face before capturing the shot. This will allow the app to detect your face and you can apply fun effects to your selfie before sending it.

Snapchat allows you to send snaps directly to specific friends or share them with all your friends by adding them to your "Story." After you capture a photo or video, you can tap the "+" icon near the bottom of the screen to add the snap to your story. Your friends can view the images and videos you've added for 24 hours after you publish them. You can also view your friends' stories by swiping to the Stories screen within the app.

There is a new mapping feature that most other parents will not be aware of. It shows on a map the GPS location of all of your Snapchat friends. This could allow a complete stranger to locate your child.

What you can do is tell your child that you must be allowed to follow or friend not only your child but anyone that they connect with. Do this on all platforms and keep young children away from Snapchat. Occasionally check the apps on their phone and make sure that an open policy of dialog persists.

Be prepared to be shocked by what other children post or do. Most of the parents that your child will communicate with let them literally do anything and post anything without constraint. Use it as talking points. It is not advisable to openly criticize other kids directly. Talk about your family values instead, be nurturing whenever possible. The influence of Hollywood and the raunchiness of pop music will show itself in full bloom. While we may sound like our own parents at times, it is only that we now recognize that they had our best interest in their mind.

The social networks have fostered an atmosphere of "look at me and comment on how great I am." Many children will invite comments from strangers, which are of course a danger. It is not only a danger to that child; it can be to yours as well. Watch for it, ask questions. "How do you know this person?"

If you do see something that is unusual like an older man, woman, or a child that doesn't seem as though they fit in your child's circle, insist that they are blocked. That is unless they are someone known to you or your child. You will, of course, have parents that confuse the idea that they are an influence and just want to be cool. These may end up being enablers to bigger issues with alcohol and drug use.

It is far wiser to watch what they do and stay in contact than to block them. Your child may be influenced by them, and any effort that you extend to isolate may just backfire. There are things you can do in that type of situation, and they are elsewhere in this book.

It is important to start this when a child is young. Trying to tell a teenager that you want to follow their friends simply will not work. They will think you are the creepy parent, so talking about who they know and being active in their life and having a real relationship is what you can hope for.

Is Your School Violating Your Trust?

When it comes to our children, there is a lack of understanding of the many risks and pitfalls surrounding privacy and security. The federal government mostly stays silent. Our public schools act as our gatekeepers. Regrettably, schools are often under-equipped, and their employees are naive about the threat data thieves impose. Generally, they remain ignorant of the methods that large corporations use to collect information about them, let alone protecting your child's data.

The first thing you must remember is that it is your information. Until your child turns 18 years old, it is under your authority to deny the data collection activities of your child. Schools are overburdened, and many of them are turning to outside companies for the storage of private information. Some of these are not upholding any sort of privacy pledge. At the time of this writing, there are literally hundreds of pieces of software running locally and in cloud servers around the nation. You should know what software is used in your child's school, more importantly, the name of the software and the company name.

School administrators along with the majority of society have no idea that spying on children is a multi-billion dollar a year business.

Each piece of data collected widens the risk of thievery. Protecting your child from data collection and teaching them about its dangers should remain in the forefront of your mind through the rest of their childhood.

If you are unsure of how your school district handles information, then ask. The question may take more than one phone call or visit. Many school administrators you will find are clueless when it comes to safeguarding your child's data trail. The system may ask you for your driver's license to see a printed piece of paper but will allow contractors and third parties access to sensitive information without a second thought.

The reasons that states are writing student privacy safeguard legislation is to regulate educators into understanding the sensitivity of personal information. In some cases, it is to criminalize the mishandling of the material. As a society, we have become immune to privacy invasions within our own homes.

The questions you should ask should come in several parts. "What is being collected and how exactly are you using that information to help my child? What do you do with it when it is no longer needed?"

Data collection occurs with young people constantly. Yearbook and class ring companies are notorious for data collection. Ask questions. Do not just fill in the form if the question is out of place. In some situations, you might just ask, "Who gets the form?" Some forms within schools are generated by outside parties. Educators and coaches may distribute them without the full knowledge of the school administration. A form shared with you and your child asking for information that is out of place should be suspect. Always ask why the information is needed. Thieves and data brokers regularly consume information from many sources. It is common practice for thieves to buy information from brokers.

Social Security Numbers and dates and places of birth are the most commonly used pieces of information in committing identity theft. If you are in doubt about the validity of the information's necessity, you should consult with the school administration and use your own common sense. There is practically no reason that any activity would require your child's Social Security Number or where the child was born. If you don't want to ruffle feathers, simply put misdirected information into forms. Makeup things to enter and watch for matching spam and junk mail. It's not a joke; it happens.

If the school does need the information, however, you must verify who has access to the information and that it is kept in a secure manner. Forms with personal information should always be shredded, not put into a stack of recycled paper or merely thrown in the garbage.

[25]The Family Educational Rights and Privacy Act (FERPA) 20 U.S.C. § 1232g; 34 CFR Part 99 is a federal law that was passed in 1974. It bars the disclosure of personally identifiable data in student records to third parties without parental consent. It requires schools to have written parental consent before releasing any student information. The only exceptions being when requested by legal authorities, accrediting organizations, financial aid institutions, or the receiving school of a transferring student.

[26]Schools may also disclose student directory information without consent, but only after parents are given an opportunity to request their child's information be withheld. Similarly, the Protection of Pupil Rights Amendment gives parents the right to view survey materials before they are distributed to students.

As of July 2016, FERPA contains no guidelines restricting or allowing the undisclosed release of student records for third-party online database storage and other cloud computing services, so you may or may not receive information about any such activities.

State autonomy, however, can negate federal law. Additionally, private institutions and schools that do not receive federal assistance can negate the federal protections as well. The political expedience of federal legation often is misreported and more importantly misunderstood. Your state may have conflicting laws on the books that counter the federal legislation entirely. In the last few years, FERPA has been weakened to enable schools and districts to share the data with others. There are many reasons that on the surface may seem legitimate, including allowing it to be disclosed to consultants and contractors for administrative or assessment purposes. In addition, there is a loophole in the law allowing non-consensual disclosures of personally identifiable information for "studies." You should know for yourself when this takes place, which companies or contractors are involved anytime your child's information is disclosed.

Many falsely believe that federal laws override state authority. It was the intent of the framers that states hold the majority of laws and only those in the bill of rights should limit the rights of the people at the federal level. More often than not, federal mandates are tied to federal education grants that are implemented at the district level.

A number of states argued with the federal legislation in that they were legally allowed to share personal student information with inBloom, without parental knowledge or consent. The inBloom debacle failed in 2014; however, the exemptions in the federal regulation still exist and were never restored. The loopholes allow information to be shared with anyone that requests it.

InBloom, instituted in 2011, was an organization that would aggregate and sort a wide range of student data. It professed that it would then make the data available to district-approved third parties. Those would create dashboards from the data giving the district an overall view so that the data could be used by classroom educators. There was no transparency in the other uses of the data collected.

[27]In a statement, Haimson said inBloom was designed to "facilitate the sharing of children's personal and very sensitive information with data-mining vendors, with no attention paid to the need for parental notification or consent."

"This is something that parents will not stand for," Haimson said.

Proponents, however, argued that inBloom has been misunderstood and that the organization's technology represented a huge advance toward increasing the "interoperability" of the many different data systems that currently house student information.

"While perhaps ahead of its time, the inBloom vision—and the tools inBloom built to realize it—remain critically important for the K-12 sector to build upon in the future," said Douglas Levin, the executive director of the State Educational Technology Directors Association, based in Glen Burnie, Md. "I certainly hope that others will step up to fill the void that inBloom will be leaving in its wake."

It is your right to know what information is taken and how it is used. It is your right to know what is collected about your child and know how the data is used. You are not helpless or alone; there are thousands of concerned parents just like you in your own state.

Children from all 50 states have some form of schoolwork evaluated by data analytics software. It tracks their progress on classroom or home computers, and it is a growing part of what the Software and Information Industry Association estimates to be a twelve billion yearly market for education software and technology services.

There are many types of software that are created by publishing companies such as McGraw-Hill Education, Pearson, and News Corp. These have introduced student databases or schoolwork-tracking software for PCs and mobile devices, and have been under pressure to demonstrate that their data is secure and won't be misused.

There are many phablet (phone and tablet) applications that are available on all platforms that hide who the data is shared with. One such application that is for iPhone and Android and a number of computer operating systems, iStudiez Pro, has no information on its stated privacy policy link. There are many more applications that are written for and by companies that collect and sell information.

State laws have made progress since the inBloom debacle and its notoriety made the headlines in the national news. It was the catalyst for a rallying cry across the nation for additional student data protection and privacy laws.

[28]Since 2013, 50 states and the District of Columbia have introduced over four hundred bills on student privacy. In 2014, [29]California passed the Student Online Personal Information Protection Act (SOPIPA) which is the first state law to comprehensively address student privacy and became effective January 1, 2016. SOPIPA applies broadly to websites and computer and phablet applications that focus on K-12 age students. It was designed to protect personal information. Even if a company is not based in California, the act will still apply if it collects information from California's K-12 age students.

[30]Prior to 2015, focus on legislation nationwide was primarily on data collected by the individual states and its localized school districts. Afterward, however, the legislation broadened to regulate the data use and privacy activities for internet online service providers, requiring the creation and maintenance of "reasonable" security procedures to protect certain information about students, and

prohibit the use of covered information for targeted advertising.

Additionally, the states introduced bills that would address the additional resources needed by the districts with the additional burden of increased data privacy and security responsibilities. States created additional roles for the supporting district's privacy activities. These roles included helping districts create and implement data privacy policies and providing staff training. New Hampshire, for example, established a requirement to destroy the personal information of students following the completion of tests. It gives students that are taking college entrance exams an option to have all of the personal information destroyed by the testing entity following the completion and verification of the test.

Oregon, Tennessee, and Virginia enacted similar laws to New Hampshire, expanding the protection of student data, prohibiting selling student information, and defining "targeted advertising" as it applies to students. Hawaii passed a bill that restricts how a student's information can be used by "operators" of online websites, services, and applications that are used for K-12 school purposes. Michigan enacted two laws, one similar to Hawaii's regarding operators' collection of student's information, as well as an additional law about how student's information can be collected and used. Kansas passed its "Student Online Personal Protection Act," which, like other states, restricts how an "operator" can use student information. Connecticut's "Act Concerning Student Data Privacy," went into effect on October 1, 2016, and addresses how student information, including a student's personally identifiable information, can be collected and used by operators and other contractors. Finally, California expanded its existing Student Online Personal Information Protection Act and its limits on operators and the uses of student information to apply to preschool and pre-kindergarten students.

Utah also established the Student Data Privacy Act, providing for student data protection at the state and local levels. It enacted requirements for data maintenance and protection by both state and local education entities and third-party contractors, as well as providing penalties and enacting requirements to notify parents or guardians before a student is required to take certain types of surveys.

West Virginia recently enacted legislation prohibiting the Department of Education from transferring confidential student information or certain redacted data to any federal, state, or local agency or other person or entity (subject to certain exceptions). It added a requirement that written consent must be presented before information classified as confidential is disclosed.

Arizona added a requirement for parental consent before collecting information about a student. Finally, Colorado passed its "Student Data Transparency and Security Act," which made a number of changes, such as limiting how "school service contract providers" can use student information and their duties to destroy data, with the stated goal of increasing transparency and addressing limitations in the "collection, use, storage, and destruction of student data."

[31]In all 50 states, there are active lobby efforts to repeal transparency and parent notification from each of the enacted state laws. The brokerage industries, along with their political action committees, are attempting to create local legislation to keep parents in the dark regarding the release of their children's records and the contractors who have access to their children's records. Don't be kept in the dark in the event of a breach of student data. Become active, find other parents, join committees, and join meetings. There is an active assault happening in your state legislature to get at your child's data. Make sure your state does not rescind the federal notification requirement.

It has been my personal experience that my local school district forgets to notify parents every year. Although districts are required to send annual notices that explain your personal information privacy rights each year, it is a requirement under the federal FERPA and PPRA acts.

I know from experience that the deluge of homework and art projects will get mixed up with release forms. You must remain diligent and expect that the forms will come. Under the federal law, public schools can share "Directory Information" about students with any third party upon request. Any third party means anyone literally. Some schools' opt-out forms can be confusing and can even discourage parents' and students' participation in opt out.

The Parent Coalition For Student Privacy offers a downloadable pdf that can replace the offical form given to your child. You may encounter confustion however at your local school where administrators will not understand somone not using the same form they do. You must remember that your child is not the property of the state or its education system. They are your responsibility to nurture and to protect.

https://www.studentprivacymatters.org/directory-information-opt-out-form-2/

You may also be notified of cloud-based services used within your local school district. The information in many of these introduces additional risks of disclosure. If this is the case, ask questions: "Who has access outside of the school district? When is the information destroyed?" You are not required to put your child's information at risk even if everyone else is doing it in the district. If the district is unwilling to understand your concerns, simply suggest using a fictitious name, which should satisfy even the most ardent of administrators.

32 Your local school district may limit the ability to opt out of "Directory Information" to certain times of the school year.

Many schools allow an opt-out period at the beginning of the school year. The opt-out period varies widely and can be as short as a week. If you are in doubt, ask the administration office a day or two after school starts.

[33]Directory sharing opt-out is extremely important. Although directory information may sound harmless, it can include detailed personal information:

- Student's name
- Address
- Telephone number
- Email address
- Photograph
- Date and place of birth
- Major field of study
- Dates of attendance
- Grade level
- Participation in officially recognized activities and sports
- Weight and height of members of athletic teams
- Degrees, honors, and awards received
- The most recent educational agency or institution attended
- Student ID Number

The World Privacy Forum is a not-for-profit organization in California that has a number of free opt-out forms that can be used with your public school in the event the one you receive is unclear.

You can reach its website
https://www.worldprivacyforum.org/2015/08/student-privacy-101-why-directory-information-and-ferpa-is-a-major-edu-privacy-issue/

The first step I always recommend is dedicating a computer to secure communications. You can use an old computer or buy a new one. Later in this book, it is described in detail. When the machine is not in use, it should be turned off. It should never be used for social networking, general email, or games of any kind.

Your children will infect the shared family computer and possibly your cell phone with a virus. Take it from someone that works in the field, this author. If it can happen to me, it is more than likely going to happen to you. Some viruses will infect other machines on the same network; it is important that your financial information, your bank account, mortgage, or retirement funds not be exposed to viruses.

All communication with the school online system (if there is one) should be done on a secure device. There are many tasks that require attention, such as managing your child's lunch account or yearly school registration. It is important to consider what information you disclose about your child. Equally, it is important that the information is transmitted only to a secure website using an https connection and never from a public Wi-Fi or from a mobile device.

Spotting the Data Thieves

Your child's information is for sale. There are a few data brokers that sell children's data. Exact Data of Chicago sells children's data to just about anyone. Exact Data gets the consumer information exclusively from the Acxiom® Corporation. If you don't know who Acxiom® is you should; it is the world's largest data broker. The average person in the United States has tens of thousands of data points in its database—a database that includes stolen information by spying, buying, misleading and trading information about you and your children.

The power of Acxiom® is immense, and its playbook is rather simple. Information is power, and its relationship with a combination of government and corporate entities make it one of the most powerful corporations on the planet. The reason you may have never heard of them before is no accident. It was a lesson learned from the pioneers of spying on the public.

For years, our election cycles have been stuck in the mire of corporate influence. Both Senate and House members spend a considerable amount of time each week raising campaign funds.

Thus, Congress is hooked on your data. Your representatives spend considerable time each week cold calling for donations to their campaigns. That is not what we elect them for, and the databases do not belong to the parties. The data is provided by a company named Acxiom®. The company shrouds itself in secrecy. It has relationships with practically all carriers of communication, website entities, and the credit and banking industries.

It may surprise you that Microsoft®, Apple®, Google®, Facebook®, and Twitter® all share a single connection. Countless social media sites, marketing, and companies that spy on your activities have agreements with the same company. You can see for yourself; Google ®it. That is until Acxiom® forces Google® to remove the links.

In the twentieth century, J. Edgar Hoover headed the FBI. His reign lasted through eight U.S. Presidents, from Calvin Coolidge to Richard Nixon. He kept personal files on the general public but concentrated on politicians. No one has held appointed political office for so long. His legacy proved that secret information is power. His power existed in government service, and his influence has lasted for decades. In some ways, it is still present today.

In 1969, two brothers started a mailing database for the Democratic Party. The company name was Demographics Inc. It became synonymous with the very definition of data about the population. In the dictionary it is given the following definition. "noun —statistical data, relating to the population and particular groups within it." Today, many do not realize that same company still exists. A few name changes later, it is known presently as the Acxiom® Corporation.

So why would anyone want to sell the names of children? One reason is to sell your child's information to companies to send spam to your child. Another reason would be to manipulate you into demanding government intervention. You can understand by learning about the history of the credit system how through regulation it caused a multi-billion-dollar company to invest in credit as a long-term profit center. Your name is your property. We do not need new legislation protecting brokers' interests.

Its influence not only shapes the opinion of our legislators. The CEO of Acxiom®, Scott Howe, proudly stated in a television interview broadcast in 2012 on "The Street," "That there is not a piece of privacy legislation written that Acxiom hasn't had a voice in… So we want to not only, want to stay ahead of legislation but have a hand in crafting effective legislation."

Indeed since the interview, the last three privacy bills introduced in the Senate both carried a common theme. The data collected about you and your child is the broker's property. The laws are written in a way to strip your right to your own information. Your name is your property, and your child's name is yours to protect until the child is 18 or is declared an adult.

Its products and services compete directly with credit and security firms. It competes with other marketing firms having the largest privately held databases of personal information in the world. The dependency of our legislators on remaining in Congress for years comes with a price, from every citizen.

The powerful lobbyists, pharmaceutical, and defense industries all use information pulled from the same source. Direct personal information along with judgments made by inferences from the statistically induced large data sets (big data) are taken primarily without permission or consent. Often, extortion is used as a means from loyalty card programs operated at a wide variety of small and large retailers. One company has ultimate control of how our legislators raise campaign funds and create legislation. It influences our economic decisions and markets your information openly. It is no wonder why we are threatened by identity theft; there are over 800 companies selling personal information about the population on the internet. Some of these get the information again from the very same sources. There are other collectors of children's information that compete with Acxiom®; it is not alone, it just has the largest collection. LexusNexus®, Oracle®, Pearson®, Experian®, and a few others also collect bits and pieces of our children's lives. Behaviorbank ™ is a product of Experian® that sells who is sick or has any type of ailment. The record of your child's medications is just another record in a multi-billion-dollar effort to manipulate you to buy things you don't need or force you into paying more for insurance and personal loans.

Information is collected about you and your children every day. Your GPS position and IP address location along with your actions are collected. By now you have experienced some level of internet "spooky behavior." Perhaps it was something you looked at online or following the purchase of an item in a store. The chances are that Acxiom® was behind it.

One of Acxiom's® products is Acxiom Identify XTM Authenticate™. Its partners include the following: Public and private universities, state colleges, community colleges, distance learning consortiums and professional continuing educators. Its core business is authenticating with remote learning centers.

From its site, it claims: "Each day, Acxiom® collects, synthesizes, and maintains a database of U.S. consumer public records." It uses this data to verify individuals' identities. The problem is that the information is far from public. Where you were yesterday is not anyone's business. These companies want to verify who we are, who calls and texts us. We should be handing our own so-called security.

It is not a secret that money influences politics. Raw information, however, is a powerful tool, all from a company that cloaks what it has, what it collects, and how it uses the information it collects about you. Our shared societal problem of corporate influence over government actually has a single commonality.

Your child is being tracked by the Department of Education

as well as private contractors. Elements of the federal government and your state departments of education track your children for various reasons. What is the harm? When data is collected, it always seems to find additional uses. When a child browses the internet at school or at home, the information is taken by online companies and bundled with other records. There is a myth in data and it was created by a very big company, that data is collected only for a single purpose. While it may have an excuse for getting one piece of data, it is forever merged into a life record of the individual.

Information in big data firms is sold as a definitive predictor for feelings, motivations, and behaviors. As such, colleges, employers, mortgage lenders, and insurance underwriters may use the information for its services.

There are things that you would not expect to slip through the cracks in school records. One example is a child that is involved in a criminal proceeding. While the court may order the record closed, not viewable to the general public, often those records are destroyed when the child turns 18. School records, however, are not destroyed and can disclose what a court has ordered sealed. This also holds true for medical information. While some information is protected under HIPPA, many school permission slips and other health-related information that would normally be protected in a doctor's office do not fall under the same legal restrictions. Many of these things can end up as data records and end up in broker's databases.

U.S. District Judge Kimberly Mueller ruled in Morgan Hill Concerned Parents Association and California Concerned Parents v. California Department of Education that the records for 10 million students be released to plaintiff lawyers. The state database included names, addresses, disciplinary records, and in some cases, Social Security Numbers. The suit started in 2012 and was over claims that the state is not meeting its federal obligations to serve students with disabilities.

[34]Fortunately, a federal judge reversed the order shortly thereafter. Parents were allowed to submit forms requesting that their children's data be withheld. In reversing her original decision, Mueller said that "given the number of objections received, and the objections that will continue to be received, the court has not and cannot realistically review the objections individually. The court construes the objections in bulk as objecting strongly to public disclosure of personal identifying information contained in the [education department's] educational records."

Brokers do not care what the data contains. It holds the data for when there is a market for it. All information is gathered in the broker's databases. That is as long as there is an identifier, a record to identify who the information is about. Most people have no idea that practically every detail of their lives is for sale. Spyware, the programs that steal information about you, were an invention of the data broker industry. Children are not immune from the activity either. The law clearly states that if a website is geared toward children under 13 years old, then the site must get the parents' consent. It is totally disregarded; brokers do not follow any law or restriction. The industry gets information however it can. When information is sold on the Dark Web, often it is brokers who buy the information. The last time there was a restraining on data was the 1970s Credit Reform Acts. This is usually done with insignificant information. Even if you do scour the so-called privacy agreement, most of them clearly point out that all of the information may be shared with unnamed partners. The unnamed partners will use the information any way they see fit.

It is more than a little disingenuous simply because most information that gets collected goes to one or two very large data brokers. Acxiom® and Oracle® are the two largest. LexisNexis® and Experian® also capture information and operate with other services that mask the overall collection effort. LexisNexis® and Westlaw® specialize in court records and city, county and state records that streach the meaning of publicly discloseable information. Experian® is also a credit reporting company that acts as the verifier of identity for the Social Security Administration. Information that is collected includes the metadata and anything else about the visit to the website. Metadata is loosely defined as the data about data. An example of data collected about a website visit includes screen size, the type of web browser, and what plugins are installed. It also records the time of day and the length of the visit, the length of the page, what the page was about, etc. Other details would include if the device has been on the website before. In games, it includes player information, how long the player is active if the player purchases items to enhance play, etc.

When your child or anyone uses a browser to look at pages on the internet data is collected. Some of the time it is used for analytics of the site operator. Most web pages have tiny empty pixels on them for third parties to track what gets clicked on. They are called Web bugs and perhaps you have never heard of them before, but chances you have been bugged. What they are is tiny pictures that track which machine opened html. Html is the computer code that makes up web pages.

Unlike a tracking cookie, which can be accepted or declined, by your web browser. A Web bug arrives as just another graphic or other file object. It can usually only be detected if the user looks at the source version of the page to find a tag that loads from a different Web server than the rest of the page.

There are many uses of Web bugs and major websites like Google® and Facebook® use them to track where you go on the internet. Web bugs are often used by spammers to validate e-mail addresses. When a recipient opens an email message that includes a Web bug, the information is returned to the sender. This will indicate that the message has been opened, which will confirm that the email address is valid.

The IP address of the computer that fetched the Web bug.

The URL of the page that the Web bug is located on.

The URL of the Web bug.

The time the Web bug was viewed.

The type of browser that fetched the Web bug.

The operating system of the browser that opened the Web bug.

The Screen size and color depth of the computer.

The names of plugins that are installed in the browser

If Flash is installed on the computer a list of fonts and the revision level of the falsh program

If java is installed the revision level and a list of installed applications installed on the computer or device

There are applications that will detect the presents of known Web bugs. Ghostery, Disconect, Privacy Badger, and Ublock are web browser add-ons that can reject some of the web bugs if they are known. There are currently over 978 different companies tracking where Americans go on the internet. Virtually anyone can create a web bug and it will not be detected by these programs. There are also add-ons for browsers to inject web bugs into every webpage. This enables any company or individual to spy on the web browsing habits of anyone else.

There is no accountability for web bugs. There is not an agreement process no one asks before being bugged. The information is plainly stolen from the user where you go on the internet is your business not the business of any company large or small.

The newest technology is called device fingerprinting. Each device that uses a browser is different in a number of fundamental ways. It uses images that appear transparent or part of another advertisement hosted on a remote server and traditional blocking mechanisms do not block them from collecting data about you or your child.

You may of heard talk in the news about a tracking mechanism called the super cookie it is a type of tracking cookie inserted into an HTTP header by an internet service provider (ISP) to collect data about a user's internet browsing history and habits. This is done primarily without the users knowlege.

Without exception most of the information ends up at a data broker and is merged with your or your child's other activities. There are very few brokers house the vast collection of your habits. Facebook® and Google® are intermediaries often in these types of transactions.

The information is used to create records that surpass most people's understanding of what data collection means. The general information name age and general demographic information are merged together to create a distinct record. It is then put up for sale. Brokers will sell anything about anyone. Your children are just records to anyone willing to spend the money. Listed are just a few of the over 61,000 lists for sale on the internet. These are not all of the list names, and there are relatively few companies openly offering to sell children's contact information.

CHILDREN
Postal, Email, Phone, Social Media
Pre-Teen Girl Magazine Readers (Ages 4-11)
Email, Postal, Phone
Email, Postal
Brand name Backpacks—High School Students From Affluent Neighborhoods
Email, Postal, Phone, Facebook®
AMERICAN TWEENS
Email, Postal

One company, Exact Data, who gets its consumer information from Acxiom® sells any sort of list. Its lists at the time of this writing include who watches TeenNick, an American digital cable and satellite television channel that is owned by Nickelodeon Group™, a unit of the Viacom Media Networks a division of Viacom®. It is a partner of Acxiom®.

About Exact Data's Consumer Database: ██ **Exact Data**

Exact Data sources consumer data from Acxiom a national database with approximately 210 million names, postal addresses, and telephone numbers, with approximately 700 selects, originating from over 2,000 different sources. Exact Data overlays its permission compliant, opt-in email address database from over 100 sources on that national database, to make what we believe is the best, most accurate and up to date multi-channel consumer database on the market. The database is compared to the USPS National Change of Address file every 60-days, and updated as necessary. And 15 to 20 million new email addresses are acquired each month, a rigorous, proprietary hygiene process is performed, and approximately 10%, or 1.5 to 2.0 million new email addresses, are appended to the national database.

internet advertisment for Exact Data in 2015

The following was published on Exact Data's website.
        https://www.exactdata.com/propensity-lists/people-who-watch-TeenNick-mailing-list.html

PEOPLE WHO WATCH TEENNICK MAILING LIST

People Who Watch TeenNick take their entertainment pleasures seriously and enjoy programs for both recreational and educational purposes. Fans of this channel gravitate towards genres of the same category and are often loyal viewers to specific programs. If you are interested in reaching an audience similar to People Who Watch TeenNick then this is the perfect leads list for you!

STATE	POSTAL	EMAIL	PHONE
Alabama	14,547	1,309	2,473
Alaska	72,896	6,561	12,392
Arizona	54,222	4,880	9,218
Arkansas	73,135	6,582	12,433
California	947,152	85,244	161,016
Colorado	83,699	7,533	14,229
Connecticut	125,413	11,287	21,320
Delaware	38,062	3,426	6,471
Wash DC	14,638	1,317	2,488
Florida	525,724	47,315	89,373
Georgia	239,029	21,513	40,635
Hawaii	20,839	1,876	3,543
Idaho	67,672	6,090	11,504
Illinois	29,682	2,671	5,046
Indiana	258,584	23,273	43,959
Iowa	142,560	12,830	24,235
Kansas	47,426	4,268	8,062
Kentucky	106,983	9,628	18,187
Louisiana	95,028	8,553	16,155
Maine	335,223	30,170	56,988
Maryland	241,406	21,727	41,039
Massachusetts	40,425	3,638	6,872
Michigan	273,537	24,618	46,501
Minnesota	104,803	9,432	17,817
Mississippi	93,209	8,389	15,845
Missouri	66,591	5,993	11,320
Montana	27,713	2,494	4,711
Nebraska	305,014	27,451	51,852
Nevada	17,912	1,612	3,045
New Hampshire	35,783	3,220	6,083
New Jersey	41,524	3,737	7,059

STATE	POSTAL	EMAIL	PHONE
New Mexico	225,242	20,272	38,291
New York	28,726	2,585	4,883
North Carolina	48,234	4,341	8,200
North Dakota	720,167	64,815	122,428
Ohio	325,038	29,253	55,257
Oklahoma	45,288	4,076	7,699
Oregon	68,621	6,176	11,666
Pennsylvania	340,585	30,653	57,899
Rhode Island	36,992	3,329	6,289
South Carolina	64,610	5,815	10,984
South Dakota	16,447	1,480	2,796
Tennessee	164,964	14,847	28,044
Texas	589,741	53,077	100,256
Utah	30,716	2,764	5,222
Vermont	318,703	28,683	54,180
Virginia	18,453	1,661	3,137
Washington	185,053	16,655	31,459
West Virginia	122,740	11,047	20,866
Wisconsin	50,281	4,525	8,548
Wyoming	14,567	1,311	2,476

Nationwide Database Counts
Postal Records 7,955,599
Email Records 716002
Phone Records 1,352,451

Information about the household of each record includes how many other children there are, income, occupation, marital status, gender, and whether the home is rented or owned. You may wonder, as I did, how the company got this information. Satellite and cable companies have agreements with Acxiom®. Obviously, the almost 8 million people did not have any idea that televisions programming or more specifically what they were watching is for sale.

The so-called marketing databases are not your child's only danger. All information is kept within the systems hidden from you but available for a fee. Who we are and the problems we faced as children should not have an impact on us as an adult.

The industry claims that it is self-regulating and has created a trade group to manage its political image. The Direct Marketing Association is a trade and lobbying organization. It also runs Direct Voice, a political action committee. In 2016, according to opensecrets.org, it had contributed over twenty thousand dollars to politicians.

To satisfy politicians whose constituents were complaining about being harassed by spam, junk mail, and phone calls, it created an opt-out system. Each consumer, though, would need to register that they didn't want to be bothered. This, of course, is opposite of logical thought. We should not have to put up with harassment and then protest. Our politicians have failed to protect the interests of citizens of the nation. All because they want to be elected to office and use the data.

You can opt out of the system sort of by visiting the link http://www.directmail.com/mail_preference/. In my own analysis of the data resellers industry, roughly 30 percent of companies that sell data are members of the organization.

[35]In April of 2017 Facebook® apologized for reportedly allowing advertisers to target emotionally vulnerable people as young as 14, as a 23-page leaked document obtained by The Australian revealed.

According to the news outlet, the document was prepared by two top Australian Facebook® executives that used algorithms to collect data (via posts, pictures, and reactions) on the emotional state of 6.4 million "high schoolers," "tertiary students," and "young

Australians and New Zealanders ... in the workforce," indicating "moments when young people need a confidence boost."

In other words, data says they feel "worthless" or "insecure" and are therefore well-positioned to receive an advertiser's message.

Analytics is the core of all social networking applications and almost all video game programs. From within a game, the designer creates an emotional state; those are captured inside of the gameplay and players' corresponding data is used in various ways. While the simplest motives are of quick monetary gains, most of these companies are building and introducing artificial intelligence. It is still in its infancy; AI will be the future of pushing products and creating new methods of selling your and your children's information. The future of AI is appealing to an industry bent on shoving useless junk down our throats. How could you resist an offer from something that knows your darkest secrets?

There are quite a few mobile apps that people use to track their children. These also track your children for brokers and marketing information. An example would be the time that your child spends in specific stores and all of the movements of the phone. It happens for adults as well; some brokers sell what the apps collect and for other than marketing information.

By now more than one of your devices has been infected by some form of spyware. The spyware detection business costs both consumers and businesses millions of dollars a year. It causes losses of production time and costs an incalculable amount of money to remove for virtually everyone. The problem of being affected varies; some steal credit card numbers and others just capture everything you do, including browsing habits, and send the data to a server somewhere.

Often consumers are fooled into deceptive practices by a group of application vendors that border on an organized criminal enterprise. Spyware is not a new word. Most people understand that it is an application that is designed to steal information where it is installed. Some companies in the United States are responsible for countless applications that have a sole end purpose of stealing information.

[36]Back in 2014, a US District Judge in Virginia ordered Hammand Akbar to pay $500,000 for selling and distributing StealthGenie, an application that was used to spy on people. According to Akbar's admissions, the program had functions that permitted it to intercept both outgoing and incoming telephone calls, text messages, voicemail, email, and photographs from the smartphone that had it installed. The app could also turn on the phone's microphone when it was not in use and record sounds and conversations that occurred near the phone. All of these functions could be enabled without the knowledge of the user of the phone. The government seized the website and the spyware application StealthGenie and its source code during its investigation.

"Spyware is an electronic eavesdropping tool that secretly and illegally invades individual privacy," said Assistant Attorney General Caldwell in 2014 in a Justice Department news release. "Make no mistake: selling spyware is a federal crime, and the Criminal Division will make a federal case out of it. Today's guilty plea by a creator of the StealthGenie spyware is another demonstration of our commitment to prosecuting those who would invade personal privacy."

In October of 2015, the FBI used spyware on a group of pedophiles. The agency calls the use of spyware "Network Investigative Techniques" or (NIT) when it confirmed the arrest of Luis Escobosa, a man living in Staten Island, NY, that was caught in an ongoing federal investigation for accessing and using multiple child pornography websites.

Various corporations and individuals create software for computers and phablets (phones and tablets). The makers of many of the spyware applications and Trojans are an open secret on the internet. A Trojan is a program or application that is often installed along with a game or application on a computer or phablet. The information gathered from these applications often ends up in the hands of data brokers. While many of these companies will claim that the information was gained with permission, spyware and its nemesis the web bug obviously bypass permission.

The web bug is generally a transparent pixel embedded in an email or on a website, to track an individual on the internet. These can be inserted on a website with or without the website operator's knowledge.

18 U.S. Code § 1030—Fraud and related activity in connection with computers, also known as the [37]Computer Fraud and Abuse Act (CFAA), was entered into law in 1986. It was introduced shortly after the movie "War Games" was released and shown in theaters. It was written in a time that only the government and large companies had computers. In January 2015, President Barack Obama proposed expanding the Computer CFAA and the RICO Acts. The Racketeer Influenced and Corrupt Organizations Act that is commonly referred to as RICO, is a federal law that provides for extended criminal penalties and a civil cause of action for acts performed as part of an ongoing criminal enterprise.

Some of the higher profile cases in which the government has used the CFAA include the persecution of Aaron Swartz and one of the pending charges on Edward Snowden. Arron Swartz was an internet pioneer who was charged with the act after he systematically copied Federal Court records that are considered quasi-open to the general public. Edward Snowden disclosed NSA records and currently is outside of the reach of the federal authorities.

The CFAA is often misused by prosecutors, piling on potential jail time to relatively minor charges in order to ratchet up pressure on defendants. As a result, they often plead guilty rather than risk trial. In our legal system, there seems to be an unjust bias toward convicting individuals and completely glossing over the crimes committed by large corporations on a daily basis. The very idea that a company can install an application and steal your computer activity should be prosecuted the same as an individual doing the same acts to a large institution.

Companies that spy on the American people through installing software on devices and tracking them surreptitiously through web browsing are both committing several federal crimes. If a hacker was caught installing a program on a server, that is considered a crime, then why is it that an organization can install a program on our devices that spies on us and the data end up at an information broker, not a prosecutable act?

It appears that justice only is interested in prosecuting individuals' actions, and not interested in the ongoing criminal enterprise of stealing American consumers' data.

The choice is yours to put pressure on the American Justice Department. Report viruses and malware as the crimes they are to your Congressional Federal Representatives and Senators. If you don't complain, Congress will continue to ignore it.

Two Sides Of
The Dark Net

There are two important areas on the internet—the Deep Web and the Dark Web. While the names seem similar, they pose very different threats. It is essential for caregivers to understand the dark and Deep Web spaces; some children actively use both of them. However, even adult internet users and the mass media confuse the two areas, so in this chapter, I try to make clear the differences.

The first region is commonly known as the Deep Web. It represents the entire internet and includes servers, computers, and devices of every kind. Anything with a connection is part of the Deep Web. Some describe it as the places that are not included in popular search engines like Google®, Yahoo®. or Bing® For instance, control of the electric power grid is on the internet as well as switches to dams and our water control systems, even traffic lights—all surprising examples of our society's vulnerability (or just ignorance). Thankfully, these systems are not searchable in the regular way (otherwise Google® could advertise a link to your refrigerator). Interestingly, many parts of the Deep Web are screened and censored by mega-corporations that block websites holding views not supported by the corporate community at large (the so-called "Industrial Complex"). There are many censored sites on the Deep Web; some simply refuse to play the SEO game. However, censored sites are a different matter than those that go completely undetected.

It's important to understand how online transactions generally work on the Deep Web. Professionals who operate web servers do so with an online address called a "fixed IP address." It is the identifying number that associates the device on the internet.

You have an address too if you are using a computer (desktop, laptop, pad, phone, etc.) on the internet. You have one at home and may have multiple devices there, all with addresses. The outside one that goes to the internet is a truly unique one, and your home router acts as a go-between. A server typically has a name www dot somename dot something. That name is associated with a fixed IP address. As a result, you type in the name in the address bar, and your computer opens the page associated with the IP address.

[38]The Dark Web is part of the Deep Web. It is an anonymous section of the internet. Once a device is registered in the Dark Web, it can see the rest of the internet but its IP address changes. This means that once your computer is on the Dark Web, it is not traceable, through a number of means.

If you ever had a kid shoot you with a paper spitball using a straw, then you can comprehend the basic concept of the Dark Web. If you can imagine, this happens in a restaurant lobby, and your child writes a note on the small piece of paper first and then shoots it at you. If you pick up the paper and unroll it, you can read the message. Of course, lots of people saw you do that with your kid. The principle is the same when we are talking about a fixed IP address; it has a fixed location. Anyone watching, like the other people in the lobby, could see your child and you but they would have no idea what the note said. That, in a nutshell, is a simple demonstration of what happens when you visit a website that is encrypted like one that is HTTPS. The other traffic, the HTTP stuff, is readable to anyone that is interested. So you pick up the wad of paper and announce what the note says. Anyone in the room that is interested can hear it.

The Dark Web changes the space between your child and yourself. Imagine that your kid does the same action, but the lights in the building go off just before the straw is used, and come back on just as you are getting hit. Each time your kid moves in the space in the dark, you get the messages but then anyone watching doesn't see anything happening. The difference with the server on the Dark Web is it doesn't know who sent the message. It is totally anonymous. At least that is the theory.

The web pages and social networks that most people use represent just a small part of the entire internet. Services like email, video, and audio streaming and connections for the game systems all operate in the open and thus vulnerable space. On the other hand, The Dark Web is like an island in which things happen outside of open space and can hold many secrets. It was created as a way to keep online transactions anonymous. In fact, there are a variety of Dark Websites that go by different names and use different techniques of keeping transactions anonymous. Some Dark Websites create closed point-to-point networks that do not allow connections to the rest of the Deep Web while others are built to allow access to the rest of the internet. These networks are used by governments, journalists, and even political dissidents to communicate privately. As awareness grows of the tracking of our online activity, many online users have begun to seek out these anonymous connections, including children.

The Dark Web has generated salacious headlines. The media conjures stories about an electronic community shrouded in secrecy. However, it's not secret or hidden; it's just capable of cloaking transactions. This degree of privacy goes counter to the idea that everything we do online can be tracked by a hidden corporation that uses it to create judgments about who we are. As a result, it affects the prices we pay for things and is stuck in a place where you can't see your own information or remove it from the internet, and that is somehow okay.

While security and privacy are the focus of the Dark Web, it invites the very stretches of what many view as the controlled civil society. There are servers and services that only exist on the Dark Web. One of the most famous Dark Web servers was called the Silk Road. [39]U.S. Senator Chuck Schumer of New York called for federal authorities to shut down a secretive narcotics market operated online with anonymous sales and untraceable currency. Heroin, cocaine, and methamphetamines are among the drugs being sold in the well-protected website apparently operating for just a few months. It was made public by Gawker and news media reports. NBC 4 New York reported Schumer said it was crucial for the DEA and Department of Justice to shut down the site immediately now that it is public.

"Literally, it allows buyers and users to sell illegal drugs online, including heroin, cocaine, and meth, and users do sell by hiding their identities through a program that makes them virtually untraceable," Schumer said at a news conference Sunday. "It's a certifiable one-stop shop for illegal drugs that represents the most brazen attempt to peddle drugs online that we have ever seen. It's more brazen than anything else by light years."

[40]The prosecution of Ross Ulbricht made nightly headlines, as did his resulting conviction for founding and operating the Silk Road. Government evidence showed Ulbricht used the nom de plume Dread Pirate Roberts—taken from The Princess Bride novel and movie—to preside over a criminal version of eBay that brought thousands of buyers and sellers together for Bitcoin-funded transactions in illegal drugs.

In our cities, drugs and guns are sold in the alleyways and from the trunks of cars. Occasionally there are stories about the same happening in schools. Inside of the Dark Web are servers, chat rooms, and other things that you would find on the rest of the internet. The difference is that it is all geared to being totally anonymous. On the normal internet, web browsers identify computers by IP addresses, the number that is given by your ISP. Additionally, there are other things that associate your computer to who you are, like being logged in to one of the big mega companies like Google® and using the Chrome® browser. Google® sends and receives information about you with Acxiom and in turn passes the information to the next partner. No matter if it is news, social networking, chat, or an auction site, the computer or device is tracked, and the information is sold. That is the advantage of using Tor; every 10 minutes the connection is dropped, and the IP address changes.

[41]Tor is an open and distributed network that helps defend against traffic analysis, a form of network surveillance that threatens personal freedom and privacy, confidential business activities and relationships, and state security. Tor protects you by bouncing your communications around a network of relays run by volunteers all around the world. It prevents somebody watching your internet connection from learning what sites you visit, and it prevents the sites you visit from learning your physical location.

There are other mechanisms that will give you away; web bugs and cookies associate things about your computer as you browse web pages. If you use a product like Tails it is taken care of. Tails is an entire operating system on a bootable DVD, SD Rom, or USB stick.

Tails is a live system that aims to preserve your privacy and anonymity. It is one option for connecting to the Dark Web. It helps you to use the internet anonymously and circumvent censorship almost anywhere you go and on any computer but leaving no trace unless you ask it explicitly to do so. It is Free Software and based on Debian GNU/Linux.

Tails comes with several built-in applications pre-configured with security in mind: web browser, instant messaging client, email client, office suite, image and sound editor, etc. With Tor and Tails, you can use it anywhere but leave no trace. It also has built-in state-of-the-art cryptographic tools. It ensures online anonymity and censorship circumvention. Tails relies on the Tor anonymity network to protect your privacy online. All software is configured to connect to the internet through Tor. If an application tries to connect to the internet directly, the connection is automatically blocked for security.

Using Tails on a computer doesn't alter or depend on the operating system installed on it. So you can use it in the same way on your computer, a friend's computer, or one at your local library. After shutting down Tails, the computer will start again with its usual operating system.

Tails is configured with special care to not use the computer's hard-disks, even if there is some swap space on them. The only storage space used by Tails is in RAM, which is automatically erased when the computer shuts down. So you won't leave any trace on the computer either of the Tails system itself or what you used it for. That's why we call Tails "amnesiac."

This allows you to work with sensitive documents on any computer and protects you from data recovery after shutdown. Of course, you can still explicitly save specific documents to another USB stick or external hard-disk and take them away for future use.

There are alternatives to TOR. Some institute peer-to-peer connections that encrypt and store data on the host device, meaning your home or kid's computer. There is an inherent risk that you should be aware of that having copyrighted material or child pornography on your computer could permanently disrupt your life.

Often parents find out there is a problem when the SWAT team is at their door. In the United States, this happens quite frequently, and there is very little sympathy for the investigative side of the justice system. Children with various developmental delays, such as autism spectrum, mental retardation, nonverbal learning disabilities, etc. experience very severe problems with the judicial system as the result of their tendency to not understand the societal and legal implications of viewing child porn or engaging in chat rooms with minors. Their social development remains delayed even if their intellectual development is advanced (as in Asperger's); they are usually very socially isolated, and as their sexual urges come into play, they often become obsessively fixated on computers and can fall prey to child porn usage or chat rooms with minors as a substitute for actual age-appropriate sexual activity.

The criminal justice system and police do not usually recognize that this population is composed of individuals who 1) have no comprehension of the illegality of their actions and 2) do not represent a danger to the community because they rarely interact with others in an illegal manner. Families, educators, the police and courts need to be much better educated about what an independently managed group advocacy group calls "prevented justice."

The implications of this situation for this group of children can be life-changing and devastating. SWAT teams of heavily armed police swoop on these socially isolated and fragile kids to arrest them in the middle of the night, and then the court system incarcerates them in the general prison population where they are vulnerable. These individuals become traumatized and then after release become designated as sex offenders.

[42]I am not advocating for anyone doing criminal activity to use Tor. Nor should anyone use the Dark Web to commit crimes. It does make it harder for law enforcement and others to track who

someone is. The NSA and the FBI have proven that Tor can be compromised if the national government needs to. If you are in any sort of doubt, talk to your kids. Know what is on the hard drive or stored on the device in your home. If you don't know it can really cost you.

[43]Lawsuits that were being brought by the Recording Industry Association of America (RIAA) and the Motion Picture Association of America (MPAA) against individuals have decreased over the last few years. In its place has come what is called a copyright troll. It is a new business on the internet with new startups and a focus on finding violators of music and movie copyrights. This uses a more profitable model where the law suits are using the John Doe approach that brings lawsuits against thousands of violators at the same time and identifying them individually in the discovery phase. A Doe subpoena is a subpoena that seeks the identity of an unknown defendant to a lawsuit. Most jurisdictions permit a plaintiff who does not yet know a defendant's identity to file suit against John Doe and then use the tools of the discovery process to seek the defendant's true name. Lawsuits over copyright violations on the internet represent over 58% of all suits brought over copyright nationally. The majority of the suits came from the pornography industry.

Many of the court cases of all types center on downloading files from websites, or using a BitTorrent applications. BitTorrent is a communications protocol for peer-to-peer file sharing ("P2P") which is used to distribute data and electronic files over the internet. It also is one of the most common protocols for transferring large files, such as digital video files containing TV shows or video clips or digital audio files containing songs. If you are really old, you will remember Napster. BitTorrent was created as an alternative. [44]Peer-to-peer networks have been estimated to collectively account for approximately 43% to 70% of all internet traffic. BitTorrent was responsible for 3.35% of all worldwide bandwidth, more than half of the 6% of total bandwidth dedicated to file sharing.

To send or receive files, a person uses a BitTorrent client on their internet-connected computer. A BitTorrent client is a computer program that implements the BitTorrent protocol. Popular clients include μTorrent, Xunlei, Transmission, qBittorrent, Vuze, Deluge, BitComet and Tixati.

If your thought is to run BitTorrent over Tor, simply do not do it. There is not enough bandwidth on Tor, and the application is not built for it. The IP addresses of users that use BitTorrent are not really that difficult to identify. It was commonplace for a notable copyright troll to request the identities of thousands of addresses collected in a multimillion-dollar fraud case. While the internet is littered with scams, the law firm bilked millions from consumers over copyright and piracy issues. It used the court and actually brought cases against people for hundreds of thousands of dollars.

The risk of having legal action for downloading a movie that you can see on a legitimate streaming system a few months later, for just a couple of dollars is really not worth it in my opinion. Copyright issues make up the majority of civil suits in the United States and a significant percentage in the rest of the world. My book, "A Right to Property" talks in depth about the issues and how it affects the costs of higher education.

The internet is not just a bunch of web pages and video chats. In its rawest form, it is simply a base for what we use today and a potential for things that have not yet been realized. There are other markets on the Dark Web that still exist that sell basically anything.

If your child wants to buy drugs, they will find them. From the back alleys to the insides of many schools the drug culture has taken hold of our nation. There are thousands of sellers of every type of narcotic, and the ultra-dangerous synthetic concoctions dubbed designer drugs.

Beyond the streets and friends' basements, there is the internet. On it, there are hundreds of websites and thousands of sellers, which sell anything to anyone including children. The internet also provides a seller rating system to ensure that the buyer is satisfied with the quantity and quality of the product. Some of the seller's ratings are on other sites when the site is dedicated to a product.

Many of the sellers are moving to the Dark Web. The ones that are operating in the open are attracting international law enforcement efforts. Just because you see a website in English doesn't necessarily mean that it is based in or actually managed in the United States.

The war-torn parts of Africa where lawlessness prevails is only one example of where sites that operate in the open exist. I am not sure how long the site legalonlinepharmacy dot com will exist or ones like it. The reputation of the open sites is abysmal at best. There have been stories of sites selling fake and worthless pharmaceutical copies. That is another reason why sellers moved to the Dark Web—customers want to be sure that they will get what they ordered. The underground markets that the South American cartels compete in have also moved to the Dark Web.

The market sites inside the Dark Web are anonymous by design. The seller's ratings are shown on the sites in a similar fashion as eBay and the Amazon market places. There are sites that pop up on the public internet from time to time. Those are usually raided by law enforcement and the site admins get to experience the justice system in their own jurisdiction. Doing things in the open is silly, just like the people who post items for sale that are illegal on eBay or Amazon. Eventually, law enforcement takes notice, and the operator gets their five minutes of fame as they make a splash in the news.

On the Dark Web, it is not uncommon for marketplaces to shut down and steal the money. Almost all sites operate an escrow service. It holds the money until the delivery can be confirmed, usually by the use of a tracking number like that used by the United States Post Office Priority Service.

Those that create marketplaces that get popular get rich quickly. Sites that operate in the questionable items category have much to fear from organized societies. In that last two decades, police across international boundaries have started working closer together. As a result, criminals in one country are relatively easier to capture. Picking up someone for extradition to another nation has become commonplace.

AlphaBay was a Dark Web marketplace that catered to the selling of items that are considered illegal in civilized societies. To understand what these sites cater in, imagine a site like eBay and with absolutely no rules on what could be sold. Often the media will portray sites for the headlines stating the sites sell guns, drugs and stolen credit card numbers. While that is true the sites also sell pirated games and movies on DVD. The sites also sell electronics that violate import laws and just about anything else that defies the imagination.

On July 6, 2017, the New York Times wrote in its story, "AlphaBay Online Drug Bazaar Goes Dark":

> "The site was hosting $600,000 to $800,000 in transactions daily earlier this year, according to unpublished statistics from Nicolas Christin, an associate research professor at Carnegie Mellon University who has written many papers about the scale of such sites. Those figures would make AlphaBay about twice as large as the Silk Road when it was shut down in October 2013."

The websites that operate for commerce in the Dark Web primarily operate using Bitcoin, which is a harder to trace electronic currency. Bitcoin is somewhat popular with a number of people on the internet and can be converted to dollars, euros, and yen quite easily. There are quite a few web sites that offer to exchange electronic dollars or any other currency to or from bitcoin. Paxful. com is one such website; there are plenty of others. It will take any domination of gift card as well. Gift cards are the newest form of payment with drug dealers offline. The cards are anonymous and can be loaded and unloaded without any real audit trail.

AlphaBay was raided in three countries which started from a single investigation. The internet is just another symptom of a greater problem in our society. The cultural acceptance of drugs is an ancient lesson that seems to be ignored by history. The Chinese government and its Communist party had its founding attributed to a drug addicted society. Recreational drug users fall into two distinct classes— those that are pre-disposed to too much time available and those that have a mental illness. Many people struggle through life with deep undiagnosed psychological issues. While, more often than not, it in itself is the underlying cause of drugs, prostitution and other societal factors get hidden by the symptoms of drug use. The dependency brought on by any intoxicant can be difficult and devastating.

[45]In February of 2017, Jessica Collins experienced a parent's worst nightmare when she drove over to the apartment of her child, who had not responded to any calls for the prior 24 hours. It had been just two weeks earlier that her daughter was found by her roommate and paramedics were called due to a drug overdose. This time, however, her body was still and her skin was cold, the needle still in her arm. Aisha was dead. The investigators that arrived at the scene had never seen the substance before. The police had analyzed her computer to gather clues to where the substance had come from and what the substance was.

In November of 2015, Aisha had run away from a Baltimore drug rehabilitation facility where she was a ward of the state. Her mother had lost custody three years prior. Once away from the facility, she reached out to her mother. Rather than returning her daughter to the facility, the two decided to drive across the country. The mother claims that Aisha had stated that she was sexually assaulted while at the facility. The two stayed at seedy motels and paid with cash. They also used disposable flip phones along the way to avoid detection from law enforcement. Aisha was still considered a minor and the Maryland Center for Missing & Unidentified Persons (MCMUP), A Division of the Maryland State Police on November 18, 2015, had posted the following on Twitter®:

Please be on the lookout for Aisha Zughbieh-Collins, 17-year-old missing from Halethorpe, Howard County, Maryland... http://fb.me/45ItaRkw4

A quick look for Aisha on Facebook® yielded an image of a young forearm covered with self-inflicted cuts. The page will be there until Facebook® decides to remove it. [46]Self-harm is not a mental illness, but a behavior that indicates a lack of coping skills. Several illnesses are associated with it, including borderline personality disorder, depression, eating disorders, anxiety or post-traumatic distress disorder. There is no way of diagnosing her motives for displaying the image. It is not possible to know if the arm was hers, but it is conceivable to assume that she was a mentally troubled young girl.

While they drove west, she had admitted to her mother that she had been using a hard drug U-47700. It is also known as U4 or pink. It was originally developed by the Upjohn pharmaceutical company in 1976. It was meant as an alternative to morphine but never received U.S. Food and Drug Administration approval. Thus, it was never placed on the FDA's schedule of illicit drugs. For decades, there was no prohibition on its manufacture or distribution. It was neither approved for use nor specifically illegal.

There are hundreds of compounds that are actually not meant for human consumption that are being taken by children as a way to get high. There are those also that start the addiction process from the doctor's offices. Graduating from dependency on prescription drugs to the underground network is not a big leap. Our current insurance system, along with our federal legislators, is partially to blame. The avenues of the Dark Web are safer than the street vendors, some argue. There is a movement of course of people that insist that somehow the use of any intoxicant is good. People who are in pain should be made to feel better. If it is our brains that creates the pain, that needs attention. It is not the drug that does anything; it is all in the brain.

If you are doing drug deals in the streets, you never know if you are going to get shot. Buying them over the internet, conversely, does invite the SWAT team to surround your home and take you away in handcuffs. The latter was what was waiting for the sellers of the fatal dose of pink. Theodore Vitaliy Khleborod, 28, and Ana Milena Barrero, 24, were arrested in South Carolina. They had gotten sloppy in handling the mail. The U.S Postal inspector only knew that the envelopes were being mailed from somewhere in the Greenville metro area. The envelopes were mailed with drugs had fake return addresses on them. Each contained pink or U-47700 that was concealed in home pregnancy kits the pair had purchased from a local Dollar Tree. Barrero had gone to the post office and mailed personal mail mixed with the drug shipments. At the arraignment, Barrero's mother wept openly in court. If there is an irony, the family had come to the United States to run from the cartels who had attempted to kill the entire family.

[47]The pair has been charged with possession with the intent to distribute and distribution of U-47700, a Schedule I controlled substance. They are also charged with conspiring to possess with

intent to distribute and distributing U-47700 and using the United States mail to aid a drug trafficking crime.

The investigation made three other vendor arrests and around the globe into Thailand. This led police to issue an arrest warrant for a Canadian programmer Alexander Cazes. He was suspected of being the site admin and mastermind behind AlphaBay. He had been living in luxury prior to his arrest. The police impounded four luxury Lamborghini cars registered in his name and papers for three houses. Together, the property was worth about THB 400 million. The Thai Baht (THB) is the currency of Thailand. That is approximately eleven million dollars in United States currency. In July of 2017, Cazes was 26 when he committed suicide in a Thailand jail cell. He also left behind his pregnant wife who was in the jail cell directly across from him.

The police figured out who he was from a welcome message he had emailed to new users at the beginning of establishing the AlphaBay; it was his personal Yahoo account.

What the vendors and buyers didn't know when AlphaBay went dark was that the Federal Bureau of Investigation has taken over the site known as Hansa a few weeks before. It left the site operational and when AlphaBay went dark, some of the vendors and buyers moved there.

On July 20, 2017, the FBI posted the following press release:
The largest marketplace on the Darknet—where hundreds of thousands of criminals anonymously bought and sold drugs, weapons, hacking tools, stolen identities, and a host of other illegal goods and services—has been shut down as a result of one the most sophisticated and coordinated efforts to date on the part of law enforcement across the globe.
In early July, multiple computer servers used by the AlphaBay website were seized worldwide, and the site's creator and administrator—a 25-year-old Canadian citizen living in

Thailand—was arrested. AlphaBay operated for more than two years and had transactions exceeding $1 billion in Bitcoin and other digital currencies. The site, which operated on the anonymous Tor network, was a major source of heroin and fentanyl, and sales originating from AlphaBay have been linked to multiple overdose deaths in the United States.

"This was a landmark operation," said FBI Acting Director Andrew McCabe during a press conference at the Department of Justice to announce the results of the case. "We're talking about multiple servers in different countries, hundreds of millions in cryptocurrency, and a Darknet drug trade that spanned the globe."

A dedicated team of FBI agents, intelligence analysts, and support personnel worked alongside domestic and international law enforcement partners to shut down the site and stop the flow of illegal goods. "AlphaBay was truly a global site," said Special Agent Nicholas Phirippidis, one of the FBI investigators who worked on the case from the FBI's Sacramento Division. "Vendors were shipping illegal items from places all over the world to places all over the world."

The website, an outgrowth of earlier dark market sites like Silk Road—but much larger—went online in December 2014. It took about six months for the underground marketplace to pick up momentum, Phirippidis said, "but after that, it grew exponentially."

AlphaBay reported that it serviced more than 200,000 users and 40,000 vendors. Around the time of takedown, the site had more than 250,000 listings for illegal drugs and toxic chemicals, and more than 100,000 listings for stolen and fraudulent identification documents, counterfeit goods, malware and other computer hacking tools, firearms, and fraudulent services. By comparison, the Silk Road dark market—the largest such enterprise of its kind before it was shut down in 2013—had approximately 14,000 listings.

The operation to seize AlphaBay's servers was led by the FBI and involved the cooperative efforts of law enforcement agencies in Thailand, the Netherlands, Lithuania, Canada, the United Kingdom, and France, along with the European law enforcement agency Europol.

"Conservatively, several hundred investigations across the globe were being conducted at the same time as a result of AlphaBay's illegal activities," Phirippidis said. "It really took an all-hands effort among law enforcement worldwide to deconflict and protect those ongoing investigations."

Infographic depicting statistics related to the online Darknet marketplace AlphaBay, the seizure of which was announced by law enforcement officials on July 20, 2017.

U.S. law enforcement also worked with numerous foreign partners to freeze and preserve millions of dollars in cryptocurrency representing the proceeds of AlphaBay's illegal activities. Those funds will be the subject of forfeiture actions.

AlphaBay's creator and administrator, Alexandre Cazes—who went by the names Alpha02 and Admin online—was arrested by Thai authorities on behalf of the U.S. on July 5, 2017. A week later, Cazes apparently took his own life while in custody in Thailand.

Because AlphaBay operated on the anonymous Tor network, administrators were confident they could hide the locations of the site's servers and the identities of users. "They understood that law enforcement was monitoring their activity," said FBI Special Agent Chris Thomas, "but they felt so protected by the Dark Web technology that they thought they could get away with their crimes."

The FBI and its partners used a combination of traditional investigative techniques along with sophisticated new tools to break the case and dismantle AlphaBay. "The message to criminals is: Don't think that you are safe because you're on the Dark Web. There are no corners of the Dark Web where you can hide," Thomas said.

The operation to seize AlphaBay coincided with efforts by Dutch law enforcement to shut down the Hansa Market, another prominent Darknet marketplace that was used to facilitate the sale of illegal drugs, malware, and other illegal services. After AlphaBay's shutdown, criminal users and vendors flocked to Hansa Market, where they believed their identities would be masked.

"Taking down two major dark sites at once is considerable, and it took a lot of effort, a lot of expertise and teamwork," said FBI Acting Director McCabe. "As this level of teamwork and coordination shows, we will go to the ends of the earth to find these people and to stop them."

Global Threat Requires Global Partnerships

The takedown of AlphaBay—and another prominent site on the Darknet known as Hansa Market—required months of planning among law enforcement agencies around the world and was one of the most sophisticated coordinated takedowns to date in the fight against online criminal activity.

The operation to seize AlphaBay's servers and shut down the site was led by the FBI and involved the cooperative efforts of law enforcement authorities in Thailand, the Netherlands, Lithuania, Canada, the United Kingdom, and France, along with the European law enforcement agency Europol. It is expected that hundreds of new investigations will be generated worldwide as a result of the takedowns.

Europol played a central coordinating role in both cases. In early July, days before AlphaBay servers were seized, Europol hosted a command post staffed with representatives from the FBI, the Drug Enforcement Administration, and the Department of Justice, along with its own members. The command post was the central hub for information exchange during the AlphaBay operation.

In parallel to these operations, Europol hosted an international Cyberpatrol Action Week in June, where more than 40 investigators from 22 European Union member states and representatives from the FBI and other U.S. law enforcement agencies joined in an intelligence-gathering exercise to map out criminality on the Darknet. The focus was on vendors and buyers who were actively involved in the online trade of illegal commodities including drugs, weapons and explosives, forged documents, and cybercrime tools. Analysis of the results and dissemination of the resultant intelligence is ongoing.

[48]The war on drugs has ruined lives and made a mess of our courts. It has created havoc in poor neighborhoods and ruined the lives of millions of people. The ease with which anyone at any age can buy drugs on the internet comes at a high cost. The designer drugs are by far the worst simply because many of them are no better than cleaning compounds. Some of these kill the unsuspecting user.

By now you have heard the sad stories about drug abuse and yet another teen death from an overdose. Addiction is a disease and should not be considered a crime. It is a biochemical anomaly and it is harder to treat your child who has a problem than it is to keep them from experimenting in the first place.

It is a mistake to wait until a child is 13 or 14 to educate them about drugs. They will have already been talked about in the schoolyard. Many addicted teenagers start using alcohol at age 9 or 10. You must start much earlier, at 4 or 5 years old, and warn them that taking drugs or drinking alcohol will ruin their lives or you could die. Children of that age will not know what it means, but you can reinforce the message when they get older. "Never take a pill from anyone without my permission. It could kill you."

Be aware of potential substances that can be abused in your home. Make it a habit to dispose of leftover medication. Do not flush it down the toilet. Most communities have programs for accepting leftover and old medication. If you do not live in such a community, burn it to destroy it. Know what is in your liquor cabinet and how many beers are in the fridge. Be aware before the problem starts.

Be a supportive parent that is active in your child's life. Children want you there with them, not on your cell phone distracted from whatever they are doing. If you can, try to get your child interested in music and playing an instrument. Go to the recitals and the sporting events, even if your child is not playing a sport. There are parents that make their child busy—night school during high school along with extra classes, martial arts, etc. Let your child know when you are proud of them. Support them in what they achieve and be positive.

There is an old saying about relationships and families: the ones that play together stay together. Do not rely on any outside help. While teachers and religious leaders have good intentions, they are not a substitute for your efforts. In the event that your child does become addicted, be supportive of treatment. Make sure they work hard at sobriety; reward them for it. Do not enable bad behavior. Save rewards like clothing, game units, and cell phones, until they are earned.

[49]Be a good role model. Your behavior impacts your child more than you realize. Create fun activities without alcohol. Never take a light-hearted approach to your experiments with drugs or alcohol. This can be enabling and make your child believe that it would be ok to experiment.

Build a strong sense of right and wrong with your child. Negative actions do have consequences. It is not only in your family; you can use examples in society. Be clear and consistent; it will build a foundation for the way that they think and view the world. Just keep in mind that being mean is not the same thing as being strict.

Be clear about the rules. Often parents make rules unclear or enforce them too severely, causing their children to react negatively or to rebel. Talk about the rules with your child and make sure they understand them. Like any behavior, reinforce good behavior and enforce punishment for negative behavior. If your child understands your limits they will not try to stretch them.

Talk about drugs and alcohol with your child. It is important that you start the discussion before school or peer pressure sets in. Be clear on what your thoughts are and practice with your child how they will react when they are presented to them. If you are in doubt you can spring a surprise drug test. If your child has used drugs, then test often. Do not allow your child to lie to you. You need to get at the problem before it gets out of control.

Let your child know your feelings about using drugs or alcohol. Most of the time, children will experiment before becoming an addict. It could be the friends that they have. Talk to the other parents and make a point to just talk to them. Talk your way into their home and observe. You can spot problem parents yourself. Your child will not understand if you react irrationally. Find a new activity for your child to do that separates them and their friend's negative influence. Sometimes the problem is the next-door neighbor.

[50]You are not terrible to institute random drug testing Drug stores sell simple kits or you can get them online. Your child may protest and say you don't trust them. Be consistent: trust comes with verification. If the test comes out negative, go for an ice cream. It works like this—if you suspect something is going on, it is and worse than you imagine. Many teens initially protest, but if they realize that drug testing is the way it's going to be, they'll likely cooperate. A test is a good way to catch addiction at an early stage. It can also prevent it.

Erratic behavior from your child has a reason. You are the best observer of unusual behavior. Do not depend on the school, church or anyone else to tell you something is going on. If you do not know how to recognize the signs of addiction, educate yourself. If in doubt, run a test.

If something is going on and you have run three tests and they are all negative, something else is going on. There are professionals that your child can talk to. If they don't tell you what is going on, take your child to a professional licensed psychologist. Clergy, school counselors, and social workers are not a substitute. There may be other reasons that tests fail; it could be something that you can't detect with your test or something else. The tests do not work on every drug. There are substances that do not leave a trace to test for.

Drug addiction can happen to anyone. It does not have any socioeconomic barrier; it can happen in any religion, and it can happen to your family. Denying the possibility of addiction in your family and avoiding the issue can destroy your child's future and turn your life completely upside down.

Watch for signs of abuse with other children, your family's friends, and relatives. There are many types of abuse—mental, physical, and sexual. If your child starts acting strange around others, it can be a warning sign. Abused children are very apt to try intoxication. Abusers often will engage with other adults; they seek power and control. They often will operate around a ring of silence hiding in the open. Abusers are in every race, religion, and socioeconomic level. Abusers are in the grocery store and your child knows victims of abuse in their school.

The earlier your child is introduced to drugs and alcohol, the more likely they are to develop a dependency. Drugs and alcohol change the brain, which in turn can lead to addiction. If you can prevent your child from experimenting, it will go a long way toward preventing addiction.

Transition and sudden changes in the home can also help create risks to your children. An adult who goes through a divorce or a drastic change in jobs, changing the time that dinner is served, etc. These all can upset your child and combined with other factors introduce your child to intoxicants. It can create the proverbial perfect storm. When your child advances from middle to high school, they will face new and challenging social and academic situations. Often this period is when children are introduced to abusable substances for the first time. When they enter high school, they will experience a greater availability of drugs, and witness drug use by older children.

One of the greatest factors of influence in society is the pharmaceuticals industry altering the perception of millions of families into believing that taking drugs is acceptable behavior. Millions of brainwashed zombies and health professions help generate the annual multi-billion-dollar enterprise. They, along with the South American cartels, have created an addicted society.

Your generation and the one before it have fallen hook line and sinker into believing that a pill can make you skinny. It was through Hollywood's influence that the use of steroids to build sculpted bodies has been glamorized in movies and videos. It has shown that people can enhance athletic ability while over-prescribing medication for attention deficit disorder and getting a generation to falsely believe that anxiety can be removed by just taking a little pill.

We are not all the same. Our bodies are not all lean and trim. Hollywood and its messages to millions of children that their bodies are somehow inadequate are false and harmful. Having a low self-esteem and a propensity for addiction is a lethal combination. We are not all good looking nor do we have perfect bodies. Embrace what you have built on your child's strengths and go give them a hug and let them know you love them.

Discussing Pornography

It doesn't take long to find pornography on the internet. Not so many years ago, it filled the pages of the most popular search engines. The links were disguised to appear innocent until the page loaded to splash porn across your screen. If you are not old enough to remember, it was a constant annoyance that forced the search engines to adopt new policies. It was also behind the pop-up blockers that are common today.

Porn is still everywhere, and the internet claims it is a 300 billion dollar a year enterprise. I believe that claim for its value is a bigger fantasy than those the videos create. If strippers made so much money, why don't they all drive Mercedes? The reason is that it is all fantasy. In truth, the adult industry is lucrative to its operators, pimps, and promoters. Very little in compensation goes to the performers in exchange.

Your child will see porn, they may watch it, and there is not an internet filter you can put in place to stop them from touching themselves. It is normal behavior for your child.

The perversion of what love truly is has been under assault for many years. Pornography has evolved into imagery that is degrading in nature and, more often than not, it violates the rules of humanity.

Some images are illegal within the United States and far outside of it borders. The mere possession of a single temporary internet file of child pornography can land your child, no matter how old they are, into the court system and your home into jeopardy.

Raw sex is not love and most of us know that. Societies all over the world are having the same problems with their children and the internet right now too. The world has an addiction, and unfortunately, it targets the minds of men and how they see women. It also creates a false impression that women have about themselves and men. Having curiosity, however, is not the same as an addiction. We are all sexual creatures. It is natural for babies to touch themselves. Little girls and boys will notice the differences between themselves. It is all normal behavior that is outside of the influences of Hollywood and pop music.

Your influence on your children changes as your child gets older and more independent. Having discussions with them about the differences between the sexes is something you need to do before the sexual instruction is given in your child's school. For children between 12 and 16 years of age, surveys state that 58% believe that their parents influence decisions about sex. It decreases dramatically after that when friends and peer groups have more influence.

Some researchers claim that 8 years old is the average age a child first views pornography. Before the internet, the age was between 11 and 13 years old on average. Additionally, the porn that was viewed then was predominately the softcore variety found in magazine images. Pornography on the internet is full of ideas and beliefs that are completely opposite of what real relationships are like. Instead of love and affection, pornography is all about domination, disrespect, abuse, and selfishness.

Today, children live in a culture where hardcore pornography is only a click away. Your child is being seduced away from your beliefs daily. Please keep this in mind when talking to them. It is a very organized effort of the worst elements of humanity, attempting to influence your child into joining the perverted circus. Keep this in mind each time you have to steer them away from porn or the influences of behavior that cheapen the ideas of love and respect between the sexes.

A few years ago, the top device used to view pornography was the Xbox 360. It was used more often than cell phones, tablets, or computers according to Porn Hub, an aggregator of statistics used in the porn industry. Its study of porn statistics claimed that the PS3 and PS4 game systems still counted for 40% of porn usage. That is more than five times the viewing done from 3DS units. Those using that device tend to be too young to have the desire to turn their console into a mobile smut command center.

Hopefully, your household will share the same core values of love and respect that is not any part of pornography. There are many relationship issues that can arise about sexuality between parents, and if someone else is avid porn watcher, it may create a problem for your child.

[51]Children mimic what we do, and they know what happens in the household. A child's repetitive involvement with pornography can be a symptom of an unhappy home. Once the child's issues begin to surface, it is a signal that the parents may benefit from marital therapy if they continue to be at odds on pornography in general or fail to agree on how to facilitate their child's recovery.

Any kind of exposure to pornography can harm children—even otherwise healthy children. The interest in sexual imagery is completely normal. You must remember to discuss it in a non-judgmental way. The point here is not to blame parents but to help them identify any problems that may be negatively affecting their children's understanding of sexuality. You should offer to answer questions that they may have. You do not want them to feel ashamed or to feel guilty. It can interfere with a healthy sexual identity.

Real life contains emotions, as do real sexual encounters. There is a difference between the machines and real life that is often mimicked but cannot be duplicated. What happens to us and to our children is controllable. You have the ability of influence, and you have the trust of your child. Let them understand that porn is not normal, that it is demeaning and degrading. The people in these movies are all damaged people. Those in the business of pornography all have had horrible experiences. Almost all of them are addicted to drugs, and most were molested when they were young.

Many in the industry have STDs like chlamydia, syphilis, and gonorrhea. There have been some who have died from HIV infection. There are few safeguards, and many of the women take painkillers when filming, so they are able to smile and act as though they enjoy what is happening to them. It is a brutal industry where the actors are taken advantage of and are tricked or trafficked.

Unhealthy sexuality leads to long-lasting life choices. Talk to an adult that is involved with the swinging lifestyle if you really want to understand what can go wrong—the idea that sexuality is confused with affection and that people emotionally confuse love with a partner for sexual release as its own reward.

So what happens if you do find that your child has an addiction to pornography? The American Society of Addiction Medicine defines addiction as the following:

"A primary, chronic disease of brain reward, motivation, memory and related circuitry. This is reflected in an individual pathologically pursuing reward and/or relief by substance use and other behaviors. It is characterized by an inability to consistently abstain, impairment in behavioral control, craving, diminished recognition of significant problems with one's behaviors and interpersonal relationships, and a dysfunctional emotional response. Like other chronic diseases, addiction often involves cycles of relapse and remission. Without treatment or engagement in recovery activities, addiction is progressive and can result in disability or premature death."

There are things you can do to change your child's perception about viewing pornography. You start by talking to them, so they understand that sex in pornography has nothing to do with love and that the make-believe sex was paid for usually for less money than a family night at the movies. The porn industry pays actresses, on average, between two and three hundred dollars a day; men receive slightly less per day. The average day's shooting includes 6 to 9 hours of video. The clips on the internet are generally 15 minutes or less. The love between two people may include them having sex. But hurting or forcing anyone to have sex is a crime. Degrading imagery is really damaging to the people in the video.

As with anything else, it is easier to recognize a potential problem with your child's behaviors than it is to deal with long-term problems. In most long-term issues that involve smoking, drinking, or watching pornography, they start out by your child changing behaviors. It's something we do as humans; we operate in patterns, and when we do something we know or perceive as wrong, we alter that pattern. Perceived guilt affects all of us and is a leading indicator that something is wrong in your relationship with your children.

Your children may bring other children around them that have been sexually abused. These children need help, and also you do not want your child learning things from them while they are very young. They are more likely to do drugs, smoke, or drink alcohol. They will talk to your child about sex as they know it, and it is not based on love as we understand it. They are damaged and depending on where the abuse is coming from; they may have lifelong effects because of it.

[52]The ease of access to pornography has created its own problem. Unlike the availability of cigarettes and alcohol, which

have restrictions on them, internet porn often only requests a simple click to say the user is 18 years of age. This simple click can expose an entire world of fetishes and sexual deviancy to your child. Before your child discovers pornography online or in school, talk to them about sexuality. The last place you want your child to discover people having sex is on a website with violent pornography.

While you might decide to install some sort of filter on your internet at home, your child can just bypass it by using a smartphone on any network including the school, public library, or a friend's home. Filters are a useless idea from a bygone era before wireless and internet were everywhere. If you have doubts, ask a tech-savvy 12-year-old yourself. There is a chapter in this book on filters and monitors.

Unfortunately, increasing numbers of teens are becoming addicted to online pornography. Often parents are really uncertain when confronting the problem and will turn to professional help once the use of pornography becomes habitual. [53]Research suggests that most pornography and sexual addictions begin during adolescence. Unfortunately, most people don't seek treatment until the child is much older and seems out of control.

There are things you can do once you know that there is a problem. For starters, acknowledge there is an addiction. There needs to be an ongoing, honest discussion about the nature of the addiction that your child brings to you. This will be the hardest part for you.

This is often the most difficult step in the process of recovery and should be responded to in a sensitive and positive manner. Your child should be praised for coming to you with such difficult information.

You may want to contact a licensed psychologist who specializes in children. You should also be open to other treatment options including addiction recovery meetings. If your child is under the age of 12, addiction therapy should not be an option since many of the topics from other participants may be adult in nature.

You should offer your child unconditional love and support. Do not make them feel guilty or ashamed. Be supportive and be prepared for a relapse: it is common, and they will need your support. Just be sure not to enable the behavior.

It is important that you raise your child in a sexually safe environment. It will reduce the chances that they will become a victim of abuse from outside influences. Pedophiles come in both sexes, and men far outnumber women in this category. Many are opportunists, and there are countless stories of Boy Scout leaders, doctors, teachers, and of course the priest scandal.

You will need to prepare your child for these, and remember that it can come from anywhere.

Protecting Your Home From Your Kids

Viruses and malware are dangerous. Both can be destructive and potentially wipe out your photos, cripple your home network, or just steal your savings and retirement accounts. Money that is kept outside of the standard banking industry, such as the stock market offers, no insurance. However, money that is kept in simple savings and/or checking accounts is protected from fraud. Some viruses look for other computers that share the same network to infect and turn it into what are called zombies—computers controlled by machines on the internet to bring down websites or break into other networks.

The computer industry uses terms that are confusing to some. Worms, viruses, and malware are very similar in function. Worms require no human interaction to infect a device or computer. If you own a computer or device that was built after 1997 and before 2016, it may be susceptible to a number of worm attacks. People that are in the IT industry are aware of this and build safeguards. Consumers, however, are not aware and are often misinformed by big-box retailers. Antivirus programs do not detect or remove these applications. It interacts with the hardware outside of the operating system where the installed antivirus can detect it. There are lists available of devices such as laptops, tablets and cell phones that are susceptible to worm attacks. You can find them on the internet. Some manufacturers have released firmware updates to correct this problem. It was brought to light from the CIA and NSA documents released by WikiLeaks.

The last time I wanted a new cell phone, I researched one that had a score of complaints and was at the time one of the ones that were widely known as exploitable. I then went to my cell carrier's store and bought one. The companies out there really do not care about the products that are sold. There are, at the time of this writing, four brands of home Wi-Fi routers that are hackable from the outside. They are being sold by two of my local big box stores to any unsuspecting customer. It would be sold right along with the cheerful advice-giving guru at the local big box store. If you do know that a device is bad, don't bother saying anything to the corporate employees; they don't care either.

To understand how this all works is simple. All devices have what is called an operating system. The three that are the most popular are Mac, Windows, and Android. There are other operating systems that run just about everything else. Those have names that don't need mentioning here. The point is that programs run in operating systems. Apps are programs, and a photo app is just a program. A virus is just a program that may be able to alter the operating system. Malware is any unwanted program, and some are just as destructive as a virus.

What used to be the case is that viruses stayed with the operating system, meaning that a windows virus could only infect other Windows-based machines, a Mac virus could only infect another Mac. There are newer ones that can jump from any device to any device. A virus on a cell phone can infect a Windows or Mac computer on the same Wi-Fi network. Often it can use Wi-Fi, but there have been instances of Bluetooth exploits. There are other ways to infect a phone or computer that include the charging cable. I have been in banks and witnessed bank employees charging phones with the bank computer. An exploit is a software tool designed to take advantage of a flaw in a computer-based system, typically for malicious purposes.

This should concern you simply because we're all forced to do financial transactions online. Everyone must access banking, college savings, and retirement accounts by using a computer or device on the web. The companies that host these services do not care about our safety or your money really. A shift of responsibility has slowly crept through society, making you responsible for knowing your balance and recognizing fraudulent transactions. It is your responsibility to notify the institutions of irregularities within a very short timeframe. This burden or annoyance highlights the risk of being compromised since we are forced to log into our accounts to check them.

This shift of responsibility has taken place during the transference of technology, with more companies creating applications for mobile devices. These conveniences are being created for numerous commercial reasons. One example is banking applications that allow cameras on cell phones to photograph checks for deposit without ever visiting or mailing the physical check to the institution.

While most of us no longer use checks, banks still call them checking accounts. The phone applications are usually a free download from the cellular app store. These applications offer no real protection from criminals, and the bank will stand with its legal responsibility. If you don't notify them within the timeframe it dictates, you are out the money. It is the catch 22 that the banks play. You need to know your balance all the time but open yourself to added risk by checking the account.

In our busy lives, we are forced to trade off risks for conveniences that can have undesired consequences. One action that you can take is to separate your banking and other actives by using separate devices.

For less than two hundred dollars, a new laptop can be purchased that can run Windows or Android operating systems. You can use an old computer in this process. However, it should be completely erased and reinstalled so that nothing on it is pre-existing. You will want to have virus protection, and pop-up and anti-tracking blockers all installed on it. All devices need such protections if they are connected to the internet and the web. One of the advantages of having a laptop or tablet running Android is that cell phone apps will work on the device. The applications made for cell phones often are much faster than the web counterparts.

On the separate device, create a new email address. You can use any of the online providers for this. It is recommended that you stay away from cable and telephone email providers. However, using them may complicate your future if you want to change providers. I personally do not use the email address provided by my cable provider. I never have, I didn't want to be tied down to a carrier email address. I have always maintained a separation from internet dependence and have subscribed to satellite, phone, and cable based on the price of service.

You should not give to friends, relatives, or colleagues the new email address you have created. It should be considered a utility account that you will use with any existing banks or finical institutions only. Set up a secondary notification service such as texting your cell phone to authorize login. Many services on the web are offering cellular SMS (text messaging) as secondary authentication. The website will send a code to the phone number associated with the account. This further protects the email account. The idea is that you shift the email communication from the companies that you save money with, retirement and college savings accounts or perhaps your mortgage company. It is a good idea to include your public utility accounts.

The email address you use is not something you want to put on your phone or have mixed with your regular email. Criminals regularly use phishing attacks to trick banking customers into divulging information. By removing your institutions from your regular email, you are removing one such risk.

Another consideration is the way the device actually gets to the internet. Many modern routers provide a guest Wi-Fi connection. By simply limiting the connection to the internet and using the guest yourself you can limit the connection even further. If you are on a separate network to do banking activities from your child's devices, it is very improbable that your banking computer would get infected. You should keep your cell phone's Wi-Fi connection separated as well, as it limits your exposure. The only caveat is if you need to print something. All you need to do if you do not trust that the devices in your home are not infected with something is turn them all off before you switch the Wi-Fi connection to the one with the printer.

Younger children are not generally exposed to people that read about hackers or participate in the activities of the hacking community. Teenagers, however, may bring them into your home in a wide variety of ways. They may not even realize that a classmate, girlfriend, or boyfriend has connections that spread across the globe.

[54]Jack Andraka was a 15-year-old behind a revolutionary new way for the medical profession to use a cost-effective, much less invasive test for early-stage pancreatic cancer and a number of other diseases. The data he accessed was made available from Arron Swartz, an internet pioneer who at 15 had helped co-develop RSS, a form of web publication that has enabled dissidents in China, the Middle East, and North Africa region to circumvent censors.

[55]A 12-year-old boy in Montreal has pleaded guilty to breaking into multiple government and police websites in the

name of the hacker collective Anonymous reports the Toronto Sun. The attacks were not politically motivated, however; the boy testified that he traded information to members of Anonymous in exchange for video games.

Your child may also encounter dark or mischievous characters on the internet. It is indeed a global connection that spans most of the planet. It was founded as a collaborative platform to transmit messages instantly between hosts that educate, misinform, connect, and create havoc. It's all how you look at it.

I believe that the internet was created for what we know as email, Facebook®, Twitter®, and a host of other services that allow and protect communication. There will be new services that offer enhancements to existing ones and ultimate failures. I believe that commerce, more specifically, banking transactions on a common platform, was a retrofit. The internet was not designed for security, and we cannot legislate it into being something it's not. Only through innovation will it be secure in the future.

Facebook® and Twitter® and the wide variety of social networks are what the web was created for. While it is not perfect, banking activities should not be performed on the same devices. There have been too many instances of these services lapsing in security. All it takes to have a hacker take control or access your device is clicking on the wrong link.

There are a lot of people storing photos and important data on the internet. While it is popular, I do not participate in all of it. Storing years of photos and videos occupy lots of space. Cloud storage is okay for some of it, but there is no guarantee that the service will be long term or exist at all in the future. Recently, Microsoft® changed its OneDrive™ storage limit. I was using that for a video I was working with, and it warned me I was using too much space. I also back everything up on external hard drives. The drives I leave off when they are not in use. I also keep two separated drives with close to the same information. I do this so in the event one fails, I still have a copy. I believe that cloud storage will continue to be an extra cost item and external hard drive will continue to be the cheapest method of storing large volumes of personal data. Cloud storage also can come under the risk of hackers or just company policies that make us dependent on the services.

Now there are other considerations that you should be aware of on your child's devices. Younger children pose different risks from teens when it comes to device security. Criminals know that and target your children differently by their age. In other words, an attack on a teenager may be just a ruse to mess with them. A virus for your 8-year-old's device could be to steal your money or their identity.

When you sign onto the various systems with your child, don't let them know your passwords. To be safe, you can use an encryption program to encrypt a file with your passwords in it and keep it on a thumb drive. Just make sure that you keep a backup copy somewhere else. Maybe print it and stick it in a cookbook or somewhere you child won't find it.

One of the reasons not to let tweens and teens know your password to anything on the internet, especially if they are dependent on your login, is they might accidentally share it without your knowledge. It is normal for tweens and teens to share secrets, even share clothes with close friends. But they may be sharing passwords as well as a symbol of trust. It can also be considered a sign of intimacy, so much so, that teens may consider it part of the relationship. This is risky behavior and should be discouraged. This can have harrowing results upon the eventual breakup situation. You do not want to be in the middle of supporting your child and changing access to your social media or your login to your bank. Kids are curious, and some are smart; some may be the next budding hacker that your child brought home for you to meet.

Often kids will bring home friends to play video games. The video game industry is plagued with malware and viruses. While younger children are more apt to play games on the internet, downloading them can offer additional hazards. These are called Trojans and were named after the Greek horse at the city of Troy. The programs are very common with video games and game cracks. Video game manufacturers will provide timed trials of popular applications. The cracks are meant to circumvent the time trial or to open additional levels. All of these, while common in society, are an illegal activity which carries stiff criminal and civil liabilities. You should discourage your children from participating in not paying for items on the internet. Piracy is why the software industry moved to the internet, to begin with. Its move to lease software wouldn't be possible without fast and concurrent access to the internet.

Game cracks are not the only source of Trojans; there are programs for download all over the internet that contain viruses. It doesn't help that search engines also participate by selling advertising to criminal entities. I personally fell for one on the search engine Bing, which Microsoft® owns. I had used it to find a copy of Firefox browser to download. I was surprised when my antivirus alerted me that I had downloaded an altered version of the program. I believe that the search engines should be held responsible for links to viruses and malware infected websites. Google® has made some efforts over the last few years in combination with anti-virus manufacturers to alert users when a website is known to have malware.

Viruses have been a problem for computers long before the World Wide Web was invented. It will continue to be an issue. Unfair practices of websites can also affect your wallet.

The game systems and websites all require credit cards to authorize the systems. iTunes, Apple's application, and update engine, also requires a credit card to access its system. Not that they want to charge you of course, just in case you want to make an unintended purchase.

At the present time, there are three types of financial instruments that operate on the credit system. Credit cards are the dominant force and carry the full protections of the credit industry in regard to fraud. Debit cards are issued by banks and look identical to credit cards and carry only some of the protections, depending on the banking institution. The third are gift cards, which act in most cases just like a credit card to its system; gift cards look identical to online systems. The difference is the gift card has a limit that you set because it offers no line of credit.

I have used gift cards to purchase goods on the internet from sources that I did not trust with my credit card. There is a multi-billion-dollar industry that acts as a third party in transactions. PayPal, an eBay company, is one of its members, and there are others. Its existence was established because of the problems associated with the credit industries on the internet. Credit card theft still remains as a constant threat to our economic systems.

The credit card system, in my opinion, has many problems that the banking industry simply refuses to fix. Traditional payment systems also encounter newer revenue models. Microtransaction is a business model where users can purchase virtual goods via micropayments. It is used to provide a revenue source for the developers. While microtransactions are a staple of the mobile app market, they are also available on traditional computer platforms such as Valve's Steam platform. EA sports platform for Xbox Live Fédération Internationale de Football Association (FIFA) is a game that also offers microtransactions.

EA SPORTS FIFA Powered by Frostbite, FIFA 17 transforms the way you play, compete, and emotionally connect with the game. FIFA 17 immerses you in authentic football experiences by leveraging the sophistication of a new game engine, while introducing you to football players full of depth and emotion, and taking you to brand new worlds accessible only in the game. Complete innovation in the way players think and move, physically interact with opponents, and execute in attack lets you own every moment on the pitch.

[56]In 2016, Lance Perkins of Pembroke, Ontario got quite the surprise when he opened his credit card bills to find charges totaling $8,860 from Xbox Live. Shockingly, these charges were accumulated over a single month; all generated through microtransaction purchases in FIFA. His 17-year-old son claimed that he had no idea that such a massive bill would be charged to the credit card. Further, he claimed that he thought he was only putting a one-time charge on the card. When the father called the credit card provider, he was advised that he would need to have his son charged with fraud in order to have the charge reversed.

[57]His persistence paid off by going public, however. His story appeared in newspapers and on television news in Canada and the United States. Shortly after his story appeared in the New York Times, Microsoft® sent him a check with a letter.

"I truly did not believe I was going get a cent back," he told Global News. "I just wanted to warn families about this nightmare."

He says he thinks the ensuing media coverage of his story eventually pressured Microsoft® into paying him back.

"(Microsoft®) made a business decision," he said. "Nothing would have happened otherwise."

A company spokesman said Microsoft® "may occasionally choose to provide a one-time refund in cases of minors making purchases without parental permission."

While Perkins is pleased to have a refund, he also wants credit card companies and Microsoft® to enact new policies to protect parents from the in-app purchasing trap.

[58]Back in 2014, Google® agreed to pay full refunds totaling at least $19 million to consumers who were charged for purchases that

children made via apps without parental consent from the Google Play Store®.

The settlement is part of the third case by the Federal Trade Commission about unauthorized in-app purchases made by children. It settled with Apple for $32.5 million in January of 2014, and it filed a complaint against Amazon, which has said it wouldn't settle over the charges.

In Google's® case, the FTC said that since 2011, consumers have reported children had made unauthorized charges ranging from 99 cents to $200 within kids' apps downloaded from the Google Play Store®.

[59]For Mohamed Shugaa, the scariest Jurassic World creature is perhaps Apple CEO Tim Cook, not the Indominus Rex. That's because Shugaa discovered his 7-year-old son had managed to rack up a $5,900 bill playing the Jurassic World game on his iPad in six days. "Why would Apple think I would be spending thousands of pounds on buying dinosaurs and upgrading a game," Shugaa told The Metro. "Why didn't they email me to check I knew these payments were being made? I got nothing from them. How much longer would it have gone on for?" Shugaa discovered his son's 65 in-app purchases when a payment he tried to make to a business supplier was declined. His son had upgraded dinosaurs using the game currency 'Dino Bucks' without realizing it was charging his Dad in real money. The good news is that Apple has decided to refund the money, so the kid doesn't have to worry about Apple making him work 8,500 hours for $5,980 to settle the debt.

While some websites are deceptive, in the way that they charge for items, many others are unclear that upgrades cost real money, by masking transactions for worthless virtual game tokens. It is done this way only to deceive the buyers. The truth in the pudding is that the system is rigged to take as much money as possible from the player who is emotionally vulnerable—at the height of play while totally immersed, in the heat of action. The games are designed psychologically to manipulate players to pay for air; to play for an experience that is only in their mind.

The trust, if there is any, is lost completely when a company decided to abandon a game completely. That's what happened to the millions of players of Marvel Avengers Alliance 1 and 2 when Disney® decided to shut the operation down in September of 2016.

Playdom was an online social network game developer that was popular on Facebook®, Google+® and MySpace®. The company was founded by the University of California, Berkeley graduates Ling Xiao and Chris Wang and Swarthmore College graduate Dan Yue. In 2009, the market for games played on social networking sites was valued at $300 million, consisting mostly of online sales of virtual goods.

[60]In 2010, Disney® bought Playdom, becoming Hollywood's leader in social games. Playdom made simple online games that sell virtual goods—like a $2.50 outfit for a character in Playdom's Sorority Life, in which players shop, party, and go to a spa. Such companies have grown by taking advantage of rapidly expanding social networks like Facebook®.

Disney® paid $563.2 million for Playdom, which is the No. 3 social game company on Facebook® with about 42 million monthly players. The deal included $200 million in additional payments if Playdom achieves growth thresholds that were not made public. Reports stated the company expanded and did not meet expectations for growth. It grew embattled in a lawsuit with a direct competitor Zanyga® over employees improperly leaving and violating confidentiality agreements. This also made headlines attached to Disney's® reputation.

[61]The games were eventually discontinued via Playdom's website in 2014 but were still accessible via Facebook® and continued to receive content updates such as new Special Operation missions.

On September 1, 2016, Disney announced the closure of the remaining Playdom games, Marvel: Avengers Alliance and its mobile sequel at the end of the month, effectively shutting down the studio.

Players literally spent millions of real dollars on the game's premium currency gold, which was used to upgrade equipment, buy premium weapon sets, and fast track their way up to Adamantium League, which was the competitive PVP mode in the game. PVP is a type of video or computer game in which the in-game combat takes place between two human players (gamers) rather than a player and a computer-controlled opponent. The hype took many in, including children. The closure of the company caused anyone that had spent money on virtual items realizing that it all was for nothing; there were no refunds.

There are what seem to be free to play games that include a microtransaction model that is sometimes referred to as "freemium." "Pay-to-win" is sometimes used as a derogatory term to refer to games where paying for in-game items can give the player an advantage over other players, particularly if the items cannot be obtained by free means. The objective with a free-to-play microtransaction model is to get more players into the game and provide desirable items or features that players can purchase if they are interested in them. It is hoped that in the long term, the profits from a microtransaction system will outweigh the profits from a one-time-purchase game. One-time-purchase games are driven by the PC market.

[62]The cell phone and tablet markets for games in 2016 surpassed the PC and game console markets and will generate a total of $36.9 billion in revenues or 37 percent of the total market which is expected to reach $99.6 billion in 2017, according to research firm Newzoo.

Children add risks by downloading applications to our devices. One thing that a parent can do is buy a cell phone for your child.

In the US there are a number of cheap cell phones that run Android and connect to the internet via Wi-Fi. These low-cost cell phones do not require contracts or even month to month service; phones all operate on Wi-Fi. These devices, however, change the landscape of the home computer.

One should note that not all games are heavy-handed at microtransactions. There are lots of titles that do not have them at all. They are purchased or are just free to play, begging the question of how a project like a game that costs over eight hundred thousand dollars to produce can be free.

Free can cost, who you know.

The Hidden Side of I-O-T

The Internet of things can yield an unparalleled future. Often people compare it to the cartoon world of the Jetsons, but I believe that it can be much more than that. Currently the internet and the world of commerce are being hijacked. Large mega corporations that produce products that we depend on are being extorted from the same companies that are behind spying on our every action. Our politicians and those in the banking industry are being hoodwinked into believing that legacy systems of security actually still are necessary. In our world of constant connection we really do not need anything or anyone to decide for us who we are. A few in the credit industry are accepting the change and offering to communicate directly with customers to direct fraud. In doing so they are bypassing some of those old systems.

The internet has changed the structure of many of our facets of life. The old news delivery systems have for the most part have been abandon and the entertainment industry has adopted completely new delivery systems. The strangle hold of the big 3 networks and the many cable channels is being replaced by an on demand instant system that is being enjoyed by millions. The ones that don't choose to open systems will be the ones that fail first.

I envision an open system that provides much more than today's centralized systems, and I am not alone. If you never heard of block chain it is the new thing offering security and trust to systems that currently exist in the banking and credit industries. Basically it is a technology that is being adopted by many of the existing systems that are used in banking and a whole lot more. It promises to replace many of the existing systems of central authority. With the eventual elimination of centralized control systems, I predict that it will eliminate the dependency companies place companies that collect and sell what we do.

When you put anything in your home that hooks to the internet it is part of the internet of things or I-O-T. There are new devices being created every day and many of them will eventually replace the static systems that are now in use. There are hundreds of companies competing for a wide array of devices made for babies. For the expecting mother sensors for fetal movement, heart rate monitors and other things that one would think would be covered under some sort of legislation regarding privacy.

HIPPA (Health Insurance Portability and Accountability Act of 1996) is United States legislation that provides data privacy and security provisions for safeguarding medical information. It covers you or your child inside of medical offices sort of. Data brokers covered in another chapter are hungry for any sort of data including raw information from iot devices.

For each person, the internet provides a different experience. There are a few considerations that really need to be sorted out before jumping into a generalized guide. The internet has different inputs and outputs, some of these you know as the devices that you use. There are a wide variety of devices and for each day that passes, more are added. What you the reader need to understand is that all are really just computers. Your cell phone is a computer, and its apps or programs add functionality.

Simple electronic devices that react to color or shape choices are computers also. You should consider what devices you have, if it connects to the internet, and why. You should consider any device that contains a camera or microphone as always turned on, and you do not know who on the outside is watching or listening.

There are stupid things people buy and the internet of things is really a different topic in a way. Its devices can affect your child. There are devices that connect to update themselves.

Supposedly, they don't connect and send data, but you really have no way of knowing. The best practices on these devices don't give it a connection if you don't know where the data goes. There are people who don't care about what they do; most don't have children and be thankful that they don't.

It is difficult to comprehend that a Wi-Fi-enabled teddy bear that talks to your child is in actuality a computer for some people. We see these devices and the idea that they can be something different than what they appear is at best daunting to most. When your child talks back to it, the computer takes the voice input, analyzes it and turns it into a command or something else. Just be aware that if a device is in your home that can hear you talking, it will be used in ways that you do not expect.

I like technology, especially the new stuff; I am a fan. I also understand that if someone can, someone will. Many people have tape over the camera on their TVs and laptops. Mark Zuckerburg, the founder of Facebook®, covers his. The reason is that some people do connect and turn the thing on. My first book was a novel, where I explained in detail how it is done by just visiting a website. The microphone on devices is also used by companies and others. Some companies are violating federal law and turning on the microphone on cell phones and computers to hear where the device is located. Some websites are using this technology to fingerprint the device.

While I am not going to state it is true, or that I have experienced it myself, which I have not, quite a few people have mentioned to me that they have talked about items they were considering purchasing in the proximity of their cell phone. The item would shortly after show up in ads on social networks. They are convinced that the cell phone and Facebook® and Google advertising® is connected to their microphone.

I will not have uncontrollable connected devices in my home. I will not let a company take my words to send me junk mail because I talked about a subject. Some of these you can control by simply using a separate Wi-Fi router for the devices. Granted, you would need to connect a separate Wi-Fi router in your home and set it up using a separate login ID and password. Once this is accomplished, however, you can disable all of the external devices from communicating anytime you would want, by simply unplugging the separate Wi-Fi router. You can turn on the router anytime you want for the devices to communicate and it gives you the control over the devices.

Remember that if a device is connected to the internet, its abilities can be altered or used without your knowledge. This doesn't mean your child cannot get benefit from devices; on the contrary, there are many devices that need outside access to operate. Take for example virtual learning systems that are now in their infancy. By using stereo goggles, and headphones, computers can trick the senses of the brain to hear and visualize virtual worlds. Microsoft® offers a simple virtual reality demo of standing on a deck of a sunken ship in the ocean in many of its stores.

Over the next several years, virtual reality (VR) will be the hottest topic alongside that of artificial intelligence. AI will have the ability to do so much more than is currently possible with technology. What will change the landscape is when they are fused together. Game development for VR is currently in full swing; it is just waiting for consumer acceptance. The point is that in many cases, you will need to have a connection for these devices to operate. You do not need them to operate all of the time; as explained, you can control when they connect.

[63]Little ones should not be left alone with technology unsupervised. No technology is a babysitter, and the amount of technology depends on the parents' choice. On October 21, 1998, Congress enacted and the President signed into law the Children's Online Privacy Protection Act of 1998

("the Act"), 1 to prohibit unfair and deceptive acts and practices in connection with the collection and use of personally identifiable information from and about children on the internet. The goals of the Act are: (1) To enhance parental involvement in a child's online activities in order to protect the privacy of children in the online environment; (2) to help protect the safety of children in online forums such as chat rooms, home pages, and pen-pal services in which children may make public postings of identifying information; (3) to maintain the security of children's personal information collected online; and (4) to limit the collection of personal information from children without parental consent

Items that you purchase and bring home, for the most part, do not fall under the online protection act. There have been efforts at suing over privacy concerns.

In 2015, a class action was filed in California.

[64]Archer Hayes et al. v. ToyTalk, Inc. et al.

Plaintiff C.H. received the doll as a gift on December 2, 2015, from her mother Ashley Archer-Hayes. Plaintiff A.P. is a friend of C.H. and played with the doll at C.H.'s birthday party as did other party-goers. C.H. and her mother, Charity Johnson were not registered with ToyTalk or Mattel while they played with the doll allegedly "triggering" voice recording and cloud storage and the AI routines based on the recorded voice.

Plaintiff's lawyers propose the following questions of law for certification in California and nationally:

• Whether Defendants failed to satisfy the requirements of COPPA;

• Whether Defendants' conduct is an unlawful business act or practice within the meaning of Cal. Bus. & Prof. Code § 17200, et seq.;

• Whether Defendants have collected, used, or maintained recordings of children under 13 whose parents have not consented;

• Whether Defendants failed to reasonably prevent or detect recordings of children under 13 whose parents have not consented;

• Whether recordings of children under 13 whose parents have not consented have been shared or sold to third parties by Defendants;

• Whether Defendants failed to notify affected individuals that their children had been recorded without their consent;

• Whether Defendants notified purchasers that they may only use the doll outside the presence of other children under 13;

• Whether Defendants' conduct violated the causes of action herein alleged;

• Whether, as a result of Defendants' conduct in this case, Plaintiffs have suffered ascertainable loss; and

• Whether Plaintiffs are entitled to monetary damages and/ or other remedies, and, if so, the nature of any such relief.

The suit was thrown out in 2016, and in 2017, [65]Mattel® introduced Aristotle, which is based on the Amazon Echo with its own voice and a few more features. It has a multicolor light built in along with a baby monitor with streaming video to your smart device including two-way audio. It is a built-in home monitor with an HD camera, white noise generator, and sound machine.

The unit is designed to track baby's interactions and is built to grow up with the child. While the company maintains that is focused on privacy, it requires parents to log into the account and manually delete information that was collected about the baby. The system, through third-party applications, will dim the lights in the room and control television volume levels. It is designed to keep track of sleep patterns, diaper and feeding schedules, and order supplies like diapers automatically through Amazon or one of its partners.

[66]The company states that "Aristotle will grow with you and your kid. It'll take on the role of tutor, friend, and babysitter, keeping him/her entertained and informed while you're not around." This in itself is a little ambitious since we generally change devices every 2 years. When the baby cries, it can notify your smartphone, play a soothing tone, and of course through third parties turn on the hall light if it's night and even start the coffee pot.

As of this writing, there are so many devices that are electronically recording and storing children's voices that in July of 2017 The Federal Bureau of Investigation issued the following warning:

CONSUMER NOTICE: INTERNET-CONNECTED TOYS COULD PRESENT PRIVACY AND CONTACT CONCERNS FOR CHILDREN
The FBI encourages consumers to consider cybersecurity prior to introducing smart, interactive, internet-connected toys into their homes or trusted environments. Smart toys and entertainment devices for children are increasingly incorporating technologies that learn and tailor their behaviors based on user interactions. These toys typically contain sensors, microphones, cameras, data storage components, and other multimedia capabilities—including speech recognition and

GPS options. *These features could put the privacy and safety of children at risk due to a large amount of personal information that may be unwittingly disclosed.*

WHY DOES THIS MATTER TO MY FAMILY?

The features and functions of different toys vary widely. In some cases, toys with microphones could record and collect conversations within earshot of the device. Information such as the child's name, school, likes and dislikes, and activities may be disclosed through normal conversation with the toy or in the surrounding environment. The collection of a child's personal information combined with a toy's ability to connect to the internet or other devices raises concerns for privacy and physical safety. Personal information (e.g., name, date of birth, pictures, address) is typically provided when creating user accounts. In addition, companies collect large amounts of additional data, such as voice messages, conversation recordings, past and real-time physical locations, internet use history, and internet addresses/IPs. The exposure of such information could create opportunities for child identity fraud. Additionally, the potential misuse of sensitive data such as GPS location information, visual identifiers from pictures or videos, and known interests to garner trust from a child could present exploitation risks.

Consumers should examine toy company user agreement disclosures and privacy practices and should know where their family's personal data is sent and stored, including if it's sent to third-party services. Security safeguards for these toys can be overlooked in the rush to market them and to make them easy to use. Consumers should perform online research of these products for any known issues that have been identified by security researchers or in consumer reports.

WHAT MAKES INTERNET-CONNECTED TOYS VULNERABLE?

Data collected from interactions or conversations between children and toys are typically sent and stored by the manufacturer or developer via server or cloud service. In some cases, it is also collected by third-party companies who manage the voice recognition software used in the toys. Voice recordings, toy web application (parent app) passwords, home addresses, Wi-Fi information, or sensitive personal data could be exposed if the security of the data is not sufficiently protected with the proper use of digital certificates and encryption when it is being transmitted or stored.

Smart toys generally connect to the internet either:

Directly, through Wi-Fi to an Internet-connected wireless access point; or

Indirectly, via Bluetooth to an Android or iOS device that is connected to the internet.

The cyber security measures used in the toy, the toy's partner applications, and the Wi-Fi network on which the toy connects directly impact the overall user security. Communications connections where data is encrypted between the toy, Wi-Fi access points, and internet servers that store data or interact with the toy are crucial to mitigate the risk of hackers exploiting the toy or possibly eavesdropping on conversations/audio messages. Bluetooth-connected toys that do not have authentication requirements (such as PINs or passwords) when pairing with the mobile devices could pose a risk for unauthorized access to the toy and allow communications with a child user. It could also be possible for unauthorized users to remotely gain access to the toy if the security measures used for these connections are insufficient or the device is compromised.

WHAT CONSUMER LAWS EXIST TO PROTECT MY CHILDREN?

The Children's Online Privacy Protection Act (COPPA) imposes requirements on web site and online service operators directed to children under the age of 13 and on operators of other sites and services who knowingly collect personal online information on children under 13 (for further details on COPPA and protecting children online, refer to https://www.consumer.ftc.gov/topics/protecting-kids-online). On 21 June 2017, the Federal Trade Commission (FTC) updated its guidance for companies required to comply with COPPA to ensure those companies implement key protections with respect to internet-connected toys and associated services, to include the use of mobile apps, internet-enabled location-based services, and voice-over IP services (https://www.ftc.gov/news-events/blogs/business-blog/2017/06/ftc-updates-coppa-compliance-plan-business). In addition, a manufacturer's failure to implement reasonable security measures for data collected by its internet-connected toys could subject that company to an FTC enforcement action under Section 5(a) of the FTC Act, which prohibits unfair or deceptive practices in the marketplace. The FBI is encouraging all consumers to research areas and circumstances concerning the toys and web services where laws may or may not provide coverage.

WHAT SHOULD I DO?

The FBI encourages consumers to consider the following recommendations, at a minimum, prior to using internet-connected toys.

- *Research for any known reported security issues online to include, but not limited to:*
- *Only connect and use toys in environments with trusted and secured Wi-Fi internet access*

- *Research the toy's internet and device connection security measures*
- *Use authentication when pairing the device with Bluetooth (via PIN code or password)*
- *Use encryption when transmitting data from the toy to the Wi-Fi access point and to the server or cloud*
- *Research if your toys can receive firmware and/or software updates and security patches*
- *If they can, ensure your toys are running on the most updated versions and any available patches are implemented*
- *Research where user data is stored—with the company, third-party services, or both—and whether any publicly available reporting exists on their reputation and posture for cyber security*
- *Carefully read disclosures and privacy policies (from the company and any third parties) and consider the following:*
- *If the company is victimized by a cyber-attack and your data may have been exposed, will the company notify you?*
- *If vulnerabilities to the toy are discovered, will the company notify you?*
- *Where is your data being stored?*
- *Who has access to your data?*
- *If changes are made to the disclosure and privacy policies, will the company notify you?*
- *Is the company contact information openly available in case you have questions or concerns?*
- *Closely monitor children's activity with the toys (such as conversations and voice recordings) through the toy's partner parent application, if such features are available*
- *Ensure the toy is turned off, particularly those with microphones and cameras, when not in use*
- *Use strong and unique login passwords when creating*

user accounts (e.g., lower and upper case letters, numbers, and special characters)

- *Provide only what is minimally required when inputting information for user accounts (e.g., some services offer additional features if birthdays or information on a child's preferences are provided)*

If you suspect your child's toy may have been compromised, file a complaint with the internet Crime Complaint Center, at www.IC3.gov.

The various companies that collect information have a very poor history of protecting it. As stated elsewhere in this book, countless sites have been hacked to date, and that is only part of the difficulty. If for example a parent uses a device to record the audio around the baby and there is a medical emergency, would the police be able to subpoena the audio? Police in Arkansas subpoenaed the audio records from Amazon since an Echo was present near the scene of a crime. While many of the items in our homes record audio, it is just the beginning for devices to be used in the court systems.

It should worry parents that anything being used in the home concerning interacting with their children is being recorded by a third party. Further, companies that collect information have a nasty habit of selling parts or all of the information. Imagine if a device connected to a website was keeping track of changing a baby's diaper. You as the parent are timed to see how long it takes you to notice that the baby's diaper needs changing.

Social media posts and other information about purchasing habits are already being used in the calculation for what you pay for insurance and personal loans. The common thought process being used by many people is that someone is looking at the information, which really is not the case. The information is being compiled by third parties, generally data brokers. There is another chapter about data thieves elsewhere in this book.

Any information that is collected can and will be used in ways that you cannot really consider. The best advice is simply not to let third parties have access to you or your children in any way.

Do not use or allow your child to give biometric information to any device. This includes facial measurements or fingerprints. The next wave of criminal activity will be using biometric data.

Your Kid Knows About It. Do You?

There have always been sick people on the earth. However, our connected world allows the elimination of borders and language to spill over across societies without restriction. The posts on the internet are unlike that of newspapers of yesteryear. In the past, it was common practice that a day after news came out, it would become the lining of a birdcage. Today old posts and news stories regurgitate, jumping from online form to paper and video news stories then finally back to the internet. The spread of misinformation becomes thought of as true, as you see it in the news and the frequent posts on the social networks.

[67]Around 2013, because it is not totally clear when it really started, a twisted idea was spawned. Philipp Budeikin, a Russian citizen, claimed to be the inventor of the Blue Whale challenge. The idea came to him to promote a page that had whale pictures on it on VK. The site is a Russian version of Facebook® and has various groups and a page design that makes it look very similar. He had hoped that he would attract advertisers to his page and generate an income from it. He instead created what nightmares are from—a suicide group on the site called F57 based on his name and personal number. The idea was that he could use the

group to increase visits to his page with whales. The F57 group was banned from the site in 2014, but it drew many copycats. Eventually, as most twisted things get spun on the internet, it grew into a global phenomenon.

British tabloids started writing articles about the Blue Whale challenge in 2015. The stories were written about the game and its danger to younger children. It was reported on again in 2016, which garnered more attention. It attributed over 130 deaths in Russia to the group, although no official confirmation could be made about the number. There were two girls reported to have died. The Russian government arrested and convicted two different people that promoted the suicide game. One girl is all that could be confirmed, but there could be others.

Two television newscasts helped fuel interest in the United States. Those both appeared in February 2017. Since then, there have been reports in Europe, South and North America. Google Trends® show that real interest started between February 16th and 25th for Blue Whale Game as a search term. The BBC first reported on it in April of 2017 as a problem for Russian authorities.

Since that time, practically every country in Europe has run news stories on the issue. There are YouTube videos currently in English, Spanish, German, French, and Portuguese. As news of the problem spreads, it may be the sensationalization that actually helps promote it.

A search on any of the social networks for "Blue Whale" or f57, f58, or f59 will yield interested people, mostly children in the "game." The lore of the game has taken on its own identity. There are various definitions of what the f numbers mean. It is not a game, after all; it is 50 things to do before committing suicide. Some of the tasks include cutting an image of a whale into the skin and photographing it and uploading the image to the curator. Other tasks require the participant to wake up at 4:30 in the morning to watch scary movies or suicide videos. All of this is to "prove loyalty." The curator, as it is called in the game, is the person that designates themselves as being the one to call out the shots. In 2017, Russian authorities arrested a 15-year-old girl who had posted herself in a suicide forum as a curator.

In India, two deaths and an attempted suicide were attributed to the game in 2017. Elementary school kids know about the game as well. It is turning into a global problem for parents as the lore of the game is available across the internet. Anonymous, the hacking collective, has created Operation Blue Whale #opbluewhale dedicated to find and post publicly the identity of anyone that attempts to support the game in any way.

The fear from many psychologists who have intervened and made public comments beyond general disgust is that younger children may be more likely to be interested in the activity. News and media are on a constant quest to shock the population, so it will absorb its advertisers. It is ingrained into its culture to accept stories that not only are fascinating but shock people into distraction.

The suicide rate is tracked by the United States Department of Health and Human Services. It includes raw data for public download on mortality. The data was downloaded and separated by age and cause (suicide) from 1989 to 2015. The counts were made by age or group and were plotted using those totals.

While going through the data, it was interesting that the number of 10 and younger suicides have not really changed since the inception of the internet. The first web page was created by Sir Tim Lee-Burns August 23, 1991. The overall trend from the death by suicide at that time was downward. On the obverse, the invention of the Smartphone, Apple's iPhone, was introduced in 2007 and Android in 2008. The impact of instantaneous communication, email, and text messages occurred with the popularity of the phone.

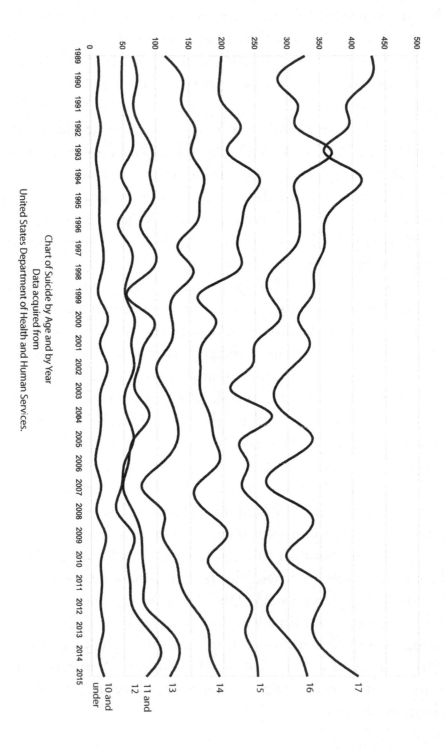

Chart of Suicide by Age and by Year
Data acquired from
United States Department of Health and Human Services.

Cyberbullying and other factors have created fertile ground for those disposed to depression. Other factors would include the introduction of the social networks. Facebook®'s launch was in 2004, and Twitter® was in 2006. It is not my intent to suggest any single service. It is only logical that a combination of factors has changed the overall trend, as shown in the graphic. It is not my intent to link the data to the opioid drug epidemic, which really began to be prescribed to children in 1990. That data in the data set has another distinction of being self-inflicted, rather than suicide.

[68]By 1999, an estimated 4 million people, about 2 percent of the population age 12 and older, were using prescription drugs non-medically. Of these, 2.6 million misused pain relievers, [69]1.3 million misused sedatives and tranquilizers, and 900,000 misused stimulants.

The other reason to provide the graphic was to show the impact society and media are having on the younger children.

Netflix released its teen drama, 13 Reasons Why in 2017 and it has been trending around the world. It is based on a novel of the same name that was written by Jay Asher, which was a New York Times bestselling book. One of the reviews of the work was published from an unlikely source. Psychology Today published an article entitled "13 Reasons Why: The Good, The Bad and The Ugly: How the Netflix series offers much to consider." You can read the article yourself if you are interested; it is available on the internet.

The novel of the same name was released in 2007. I have my own personal doubts of its encouragement in the general population and its influence on the suicide numbers. You are your own judge. Don't expect that the media, print, television or social media will talk about any ill effect on society.

If you or your child is suicidal, in crisis, or know someone who is, there is help available.

National Suicide Prevention Hotline: 800-273-TALK

Suicide & Depression Hotline—Covenant House: 800-999-9999

Suicide Prevention Services Depression Hotline: 630-482-9696

The Samaritans: 0845 790 9090

Teaching Your Children To Encrypt

There is a battle raging in society over the use of encryption. Most have heard the word, and it is very important that you as a caregiver understand what it is and what it is not. It is the most over-used word in technology. Most of society, including the genius gurus at the big box stores, are clueless.

Encryption is a method of protecting data from people that you don't want to be able to see it. For example, when you use a credit card on a movie ticket site, your device encrypts the information. It is so others cannot steal the personal data that is being transferred.

You use it when you are banking online and you may have it on your cell phone. Encryption techniques are transparent and you use them all the time. Many people use the terms encryption or cryptography interchangeably. [70]They are different: cryptography is the science of secret communication, and encryption refers to one component of that science.

Creating a cipher is something you may have done as a child. In the time before computers, it was commonplace for children to play with decoder rings that came in cereal boxes.

The most common cipher is substitution or transposition.

A simple example is counting the letters of the alphabet. The letter A is first and B is second and so on. As a child you may have sent a message to a friend that substituted letters for numbers. That was a substitution cipher. [71]Transposition ciphers are a bit different to substitution ciphers. In a transposition cipher, the letters are just moved around. A simple example is to just reverse the letters in each word. This is an example, "SIHT SI NA ELPMAXE."

In the example, the letters were shifted. Believe it or not most of the encryption methods that are used today are not that difficult to decipher—that is, read the communications, which is because the keys are publicly known.

I believe that it is possible to secure the banking industry and credit card transactions. I just don't think that the industry really cares about real security. It would rather make you dependent on its system and scare you with the threat of theft if you left it. The same goes for the credit industry that sells a system of bad risk based on a fear of the bad guy. Organized criminals can pay their bills on time, does that not make them a threat?

There are several methods of encrypting communication that you encounter all of the time. When you use a web browser and open a site that is protected with https, it is an encrypted form of communication. If you have the newer chip and pin credit card, the chip is encrypted, and the communication back to the credit merchant back is also encrypted.

These use what is called a shared key strategy. They key is given to you right from the website, or is known inside of the little box that you slide the card into. Not only is the key shared in the open, but anyone that is a criminal can also see the key and use it. What really protects your web session are an arbitrary number, mixed with your physical IP address and the exact time. These are used in a cookie that the device uses. Cookies are nothing more than simple files that exist where the web browser can write to it. It is a scratch pad, like when you grab a piece of paper and write notes to yourself.

You may have heard over and over why it is a bad idea to use public Wi-Fi. Principally it is because of what was just explained. If you are doing banking anyone on the same router can mimic your connection. This holds true on practically all web https connections. It is also true when using your credit card online.

The chapter on protecting yourself from your children details what you should do at home, and how you can separate your communication from malware on your children's devices.

There are other forms of encryption. There are programs that you can use to encrypt the files on your computer and your phone. You should use both and you should teach your children to encrypt their phones. The simple reason is they are children and will lose the thing. Most phones, Android and iPhone, have encryption built into their operating system. Your child may have things on their phone that could be a source of embarrassment with other children. It is normal, after all, who hasn't sent a text message that is personal in nature? While installing encryption on your child's devices you may encounter the tech industry butting into its simplistic biometric junk at you.

I believe that using fingerprints and facial recognition for decryption are generally a bad idea. The reason is that the companies that promote its use have all been hacked. Additionally, some of the companies that started in the biometric racket have ceased to exist. All of the data that it collected was sold. So while millions of people have given their fingerprints and pictures of their faces to make it simple for themselves, countless thieves have the same information. Devices that use these can be broken into without the owner's permission. Only passwords or pin codes that limit the number of attempts should be used.

The news media sensationalized the iPhone encryption issue as a problem for the state. In December of 2015, a terrorist attack occurred in San Bernardino, California, that killed 14 people and injured 22. The FBI recovered an iPhone 5C that it claimed belonged to the company that one of the attackers worked for. It wanted Apple to unlock the phone and give the FBI the data from it. As a result, it pitted the question of encrypting phones and technology into the public spotlight.

[72]First, there is not a safe cell phone; all cell phones can be remotely hacked. There is a flaw in the telecommunications network called SS7, a global network that cellular carriers use to communicate with one another when directing calls, texts and internet data.

Several decades ago when only a few large carriers controlled the bulk of global phone traffic, they built the SS7 network. Now there are thousands of companies that use the SS7 to provide service to billions of phones and other mobile devices.

Any phone can be injected with malware, geo tracked or its calls listened to. This is not something that our government or the cellular industry wants to admit to the marketplace. You and your child should understand that for enough money, anyone can tap quite easily into the cellular system. A bright 14-year-old could also gain access to the system at any time. The message here is simple: don't trust phones for communicating sensitive information.

Currently, there are professional spy organizations that sell geolocation data to the system openly. It makes any person's position on the planet a selling point. These companies market the information primarily to governmental spy organizations. It is not really something that any consumer can afford to purchase.

The phone that the FBI recovered was locked with a four-digit password and was set to eliminate all its data after ten failed password attempts. It had contacted Apple to create software and inject it into the phone to unlock the device. Apple declined to create the software, and a hearing was scheduled for March 22, 2016. However, a day before the hearing was supposed to happen, the government obtained a delay, saying they had found a third party able to assist in unlocking the iPhone and, on March 28, it announced that the FBI had unlocked the iPhone and withdrew its request.

There are third-party applications that can encrypt your data. Many of the cloud sharing apps have been compromised. Your children are well aware that many of the Hollywood stars have had their phones or the cloud sharing applications compromised, allowing their nude pictures to be shared by millions.

The way that you protect information, such as pictures in cloud apps like Microsoft® One Drive™ Dropbox® or iCloud™, is to encrypt the file using a third-party encryption app. This way the file is unreadable, without knowing how to decrypt it.

While I am not going to endorse any particular application for encrypting files, there are a few things that you may want to consider based on the brands of your devices. There are applications that are cross-platform, meaning that they will work with Mac, Windows, Android, and iPhone.

I have found that I don't really require individual things that need to be encrypted on my phone anyway, so I use an application to encrypt just the computer. What I encrypt is anything that is personal in nature. Of course, I did not encrypt this book, while I am sharing access to it with editors.

You should encrypt things that are important to you, things that contain information like Social Security Numbers, bank statements or things about your children. I use one of the cloud applications for backup of my information. I also use external drives that use a different encryption application than my main one.

Many of the removable devices on the market today offer encryption. You should pick up one of these devices and make a copy of all of your photos, correspondence and put it on the backup device. Lots of people argue that the cloud offers the same thing. That is very far from the truth. External drives offer long-term storage and will last for very many years. External drives are inexpensive and when not in use, leave them unplugged. Most hard drives that are made today only last a few years when they are used constantly. Websites and technology changes don't depend on any service to remain free or even to still be there in a decade.

Encryption is important for you to learn, and important for your children. By the time they are your age, they will be using encryption as a matter of course. They may remember now when it was just an option. Things get stolen even if you don't share your computer with anyone. All someone needs is a few minutes at your keyboard to retrieve anything that they want. Passwords no matter how difficult or complex can be bypassed with ease. This is true with Windows and Mac-based computers.

There are two different strategies when encrypting computers. One is encrypting the entire thing, including the operating system. Generally, that is what occurs when you encrypt a cell phone. The problem you might experience is hard drive failure which would make the drive unreadable. The advantage is simple: the machine will not start if the password is not known. The other approach is to encrypt the sensitive files only. Of course, anyone can read the unencrypted files and use the browser to download malware. This is true on an encrypted device as well. If you give your phone to someone else they can install malware for you, and then hand it back.

So what about the passwords? By now you have been told that you need to have a password for each thing you use. Every site that you visit wants its own login with a unique password. How can you keep track of it all? The answer is encrypting them. There are many ways to store web passwords, and most web browsers have the ability to store passwords inside the browser. Google® will even sync the passwords for you if you let it.

Some malware will steal the data files directly from the web browser. There are sites online that serve as password storage systems; most of them have been hacked already. Then there are the password managers that you can put on your computer. Most of them have been hacked also. If you do it yourself, it is unlikely that you will have any problems.

The first step is getting a few removable flash drives. You will want to get one for yourself and one for each child. You can add a layer of protection to the devices if you buy a type that supports encryption. They are more expensive than a common flash drive. You can buy the less expesive one if you will not need a lot of space.

Install an encryption program on your computer. Once you go through the setup of the program, it will ask you for a password or pin code. Your password should contain numbers, upper and lower case letters and symbols. This is the password or pin that you will have to remember. You should make it strong and at least 12 characters long. A password is really the wrong word to use in today's society. The expression should really be passphrase.

Most standalone programs will allow to you make a backup of your key in the event your computer no longer functions, and you have to reinstall. You should copy both the key and the installation program to a separate flash drive then you are going to use for your passwords. If you are sharing your computer with your children, switch over to their account and follow the same steps. Let them create the password, with the same rules. You can use the same flash drive for their key(s), you may want to label them, so they do not get mixed up. Put the flash drive with your keys in a safe place. It will be the only way to get your files back if you forget the password.

There is a word of caution about any file on your computer that is sensitive regarding malware. Often the programs are given the same right as the user. As a result, malware may be able to read the file you use for passwords. It is unlikely, but it is possible.

Your passwords now can be created using the program of your choice—Text editor, write, notepad, you can pick. You want to save the file encrypted to a flash drive. Anytime you need a password, plug the drive in. Just remember that you must eject the drive before you remove it, as not doing so may corrupt the drive.

For an added layer of protection, there are USB flash drives that have encryption built in. Cheaper ones that have password protection are not the same. The password is stored on the drive and is no better than putting a deadbolt on a screen door.

Security is not a joke; it keeps away hackers and other bad actors. Remember that people that steal are lazy. It really comes down to the low-hanging fruit principal: the harder it is for you, the less likely they will be interested in you.

Planning Your Child's Future

In other chapters of this book, it is suggested that children not use real names when establishing a web presence or when creating social media accounts. Companies and colleges are using social media and searching for profiles of your children. With this in mind, think of social media accounts as a sales portfolio, and you should groom the account as such. There is an advantage to having multiple emails and social media accounts as well. Just make sure the one associated with the profile you want to build is registered to a smartphone and a computer. The one that your child will really use should not have their real name; never allow them to use the same computer that the other profile is accessed from. You should start this process when your child is at least 14 years of age.

Your child will stand apart since most other children will have an abundance of images that they will need to remove. You should take the time and help your child craft exactly what you want the companies and colleges to find. Imagine the advantage of having pictures of school events, awards, and extracurricular activities neatly displayed for anyone to appreciate. The reason for starting at 14 is it will have enough information and posts by the time they are 18 to make it look completely legitimate; after all, it is real.

Embellishment is completely optional. To build a flowing social profile on the networks takes time; each photograph or post has a corresponding time and date stamp. While no one will know or could possibly go back and check events' dates in the past, someone looking at the profile may notice if all of the images were uploaded the same day. Thus, it is important to create posts and images over an extended period of time. You might want to create a calendar event to remind yourself to produce a posting at least every two weeks for a child under 16, and once a week until they graduate from college. Future employers will also look at the same profile, at the same information, all displaying a childhood filled with personal achievement.

The social profiles you create will be the sales tool for your child's future. Think of it as your child's digital portfolio. You should keep it completely private and change the account settings to public around the time your child is in 11th grade or just before they start looking at colleges. When people look on the internet for profiles, often they stop looking when they believe that they have found the right one.

Often teenagers forget about their digital footprint. Especially when vacation time comes, it is important to remind them that future employers may snoop on what they have posted. What most parents and children don't understand is that when images posted on Facebook®, for example, are deleted, it is not the same as deleting a file on your home device. An online image is just set not to show anymore. Many of the images are kept and stored forever and are accessible from Facebook® from other sources. The reason I say this is that embarrassing images may come up in their future and be used against them in the corporate or political arena.

Many college admissions offices are using social media profiles and relying on digital reputations to discern the character of their applicants. The overview of social media does not just include reviewing applications but is used in the admissions process along with GPA and testing scores.

It is not a secret that colleges do this and there are plenty of stories about students being turned down for admission. It can be for anything—saying disparaging things, using profanity, or having a belief that is not in concert with the popular view. Of course, the college would never admit that political views or the parent's political views would limit access to higher education.

[73]On June 6, 2017, Forbes published the following:

At least 10 students accepted to Harvard have had their offers rescinded after administrators discovered offensive posts in a private, online Facebook® messaging group, the Harvard Crimson reported Sunday. The Holocaust, child abuse, sexual assault, as well as posts that denigrated minority groups, were all fair game in the meme-focused private group chat at one point called "Harvard Memes for Horny Bourgeois Teens."

One post called the hypothetical hanging of a Mexican child "piñata time," the Crimson reported. Others allegedly mocked children of drone strike-victims and those with disabilities. Harvard does not comment on individual applicants' admission statuses, but incoming students are explicitly told upon receiving an offer that behavior that brings into question their moral character can jeopardize their admission.

Depending on what your child's future holds, how far you want your child to succeed really depends on you. It depends on your planning and your expectations. I personally believe that we can be whatever we want to in this country and the only limits we face are some of our own making and the creeping role of big data.

To succeed in anything, you need to plan for it. In your child's case, you plan for their future.

There are things the admission people are looking for, achievement awards, evidence of leadership, extracurricular activities, just to name a few. It doesn't take much to stage photographs and insert them into the social media account. It can be a fun activity, and they are not things that you will write down on any application. All that is being suggested is that if schools want to spy on your child and make decisions, then why not give them a show. Take a picture with the fire department, EMTs, police, or even with local government officials. Pose feeding the homeless or directing someone to do a task.

Many of the schools throughout the country promote political correctness. Keep this in mind if you are going to use photographs in your child's social profile. No matter what your personal political beliefs are, see what is currently being embraced by those in the major universities. You should do this even while your child is young and create photographs to reinforce the idea that your beliefs match what is popular in the news.

A word of caution—the banking industry and the insurance industry are rather dry and conservative in the HR departments. Political action and protest images are not anything that you want in the profile. It may create brownie points for some admission departments, but in general, corporate America wants to see the cookie cutter images. Some industries won't care what is on the internet. Many will not even look at anything.

In the event you don't want to take the time and trust that your child will manage their own profile, instruct them to think twice before posting revealing photos or offensive memes. Never post lewd comments; it can help retain clean profiles. You should keep track of what they are doing, who they friend or follow to keep track of what they are posting. Suggest to your child to think before posting images: "Would you want your grandparents to see that?"

[74]91 percent of teens use mobile devices and use the internet daily. [75]40 percent of college admissions officers admit to looking at social profiles to influence an admission decision, and 30 percent found a reason to reject an application based on information posted in the social profile. [76]93 percent of corporate HR departments look at social networking profiles of young people before making a hiring decision.

You should have an open discussion on what positive and negative posts are. Keep in mind that someday someone will be making judgments about your child based on what is being posted.

[76]You should consider what you post online and how you represent yourself to people that are not familiar with you. In the perspective of people that browse your social media (such as your future employers), what is posted online is sometimes the only form of representation to identify your values and moral standing. Corporations do watch social media posts. It is not uncommon for corporations to fire employees for making disparaging comments on social networks.

Let your children know that others will be watching their posts. Before they post anything, ask if they think the post would be okay with teachers or future employers viewing what they post. Anything that they do post should be private to only their friends; never post to the entire earth.

The internet was not created to limit free speech nor is it in place for large corporations to spy on our actions. Having an online presence is something that you should not be afraid of. It can be important for you to guide your children through constructing an online presence. In a society that preys into our actions and judges what we do, creatively constructing impressions is paramount.

There are actions that kids can take that can limit their future. Social media posts that promote illegal drug or alcohol use, for example, are not things the employers or college admission people want to see. The extensive use of bad grammar and profanity are frowned upon; sexual situations and any other reference to counter-culture should be avoided. Remember that political correctness is embraced within most universities and their administrations; never post anything that runs afoul of the belief system.

At around 16 years old, create social media posts, videos, and create a blog. Your child should post to one of these at least once a week. Work with your child and plan the posts. They can be on any topic that your child wishes, just remember to keep political views in alignment with that of the university. Of the things that are posted, one or two will be looked at, read, or watched; most of the others will be skipped over. You want to make sure that each is complete, concise, and drives a point along with a solution near the end. There will be times in the summer months that it is not possible to post anything; no one will notice.

There is a subtle reason to get your child to write and create videos, and it is not just for future employers and college admission officers to find it. Good writing takes practice, so does the spoken word. Both of these take abilities that your child will use in their future. They are the fundamental skills that are not being taught in many classrooms. The skills of being an effective speaker or writer are desired in corporate settings.

There are thousands of people on the internet that create blog posts and videos that rant and complain. It is so pervasive that anyone is suggesting even a simplistic solution to what they are communicating stands apart. The idea of this exercise is to make your child stand out and separate from other kids doing the same type of things. The reason to do both, and they can be on overlapping topics, is that most people only do one medium and you want to project the over-achiever. People have a personal bias—some read, and some consume video.

Plan with your child. Do not leave this task to them to complete on their own. Help them with what they are going to create, what will be covered, and the wording used in the video or blog. Try to use an expanded vocabulary. When creating videos make sure your child projects being happy, smile, and be upbeat. Make sure that care is taken with spelling and grammar and mistakes are kept to a minimum in anything written. Think of subjects that would appeal to the audience of 25 to 30 years old and female. There are some men in the field, but most that will be looking at background entries will be younger female staff members.

The overall objective is to project your child as a likable and approachable person. This investment in time should not be taken lightly. As mentioned earlier, admission officers who look at what has been created will make a judgment based on a few seconds of video or even other factors outside of your control. There have been reports of admission officers who would not accept applicants from a rival sports city. There is no oversight nor is there a second shot; the admission process and the judgments made about your child determine parts of their future.

Around six months before starting the process of picking schools, make certain the permissions are set to public on the social networks. Your child should open new accounts on other social networks as well and cross-post up to 10 prior posts that they are particularly proud of. This action will get the search engines to index the posts and make your child findable. You can check the search engine yourself using any computer or device that is not yours. Personalization in the search system creates a false bias to search results. What you get is not the same as a stranger. One way to check is to stop in a store like a cell phone or electronics retailer that has display units and search for your child's name using that device. Starting this process before the admission process will allow you to make corrections if any are needed.

[77]Facebook® purchased Instagram in 2012. Photos of people on both systems employ facial recognition scanners. Most people do not realize that Facebook® keeps how people are connected along with the most advanced facial image index. You should reserve the use of Facebook® and Instagram for your child's portfolio. There are many other social networks that they can play on.

Your child may attempt to create another account under the alternative name on the system but don't be surprised if they lock a profile out. Facebook® will lock out profiles if it detects a duplicate. It is possible that it will lock out the wrong one; it is better to just use other systems and reserve that one for your presentation.

Bibliography

1 PureSight Online Child Safety (2011) Online Predators—Statistics Retrieved from http://puresight.com/ Pedophiles/Online-Predators/online-predators-statistics.html (Aug 15,2017)

2 Texting And Sexting | Shazam Kianpour & Associates, P.c, http://www.shazamlaw.com/Sex-Crimes-Attorney-in-Denver/Texting-and-Sexting.shtml (accessed June 25, 2017).

3 Sextortion: A growing crime in the digital world (JUN 24, 2016) Retrieved from http://blog.missingkids.com/ (Aug 17,2017)

4 Wolak J, Mitchell K, Finkelhor D. Online victimization: 5 years later. Alexandria, VA: National Center for Missing & Exploited Children; 2006. Retrieved from http://www.unh.edu/ccrc/pdf/CV138.pdf. (AUG 16,2017)

5 Sex offenders booted from Xbox Live, other game networks (APR 06, 2012) Retrieved from http://www.foxnews.com/tech/2012/04/06/sex-offenders-booted-from-xbox-live-other-game-networks.html (AUG 16,2017)

6 Operation Brokenheart Iv Nr 17183rh - Los Angeles Police .., http://www.lapdonline.org/home/news_view/62525 (accessed June 25, 2017).

7   Nearly 200 Child Predators Arrested In Massive Southland Raid: Police (JUN 16,2017) https://patch.com/california/hollywood/nearly-200-child-predators-arrested-massive-southland-raid-police (AUG 28, 2017)

8 Operation Brokenheart IV (JUN 16, 2017) http://lapdblog.typepad.com/lapd_blog/2017/06/operation-brokenheart-iv.html (AUG 28,2017)

9 About Protecting Your Kids — Fbi, https://www.fbi.gov/scams-and-safety/protecting-your-kids (accessed June 25, 2017).

10 Difference Between a Troll & a Cyberbully by Micah McDunnigan (MAR 27,2013) http://itstillworks.com/difference-between-troll-cyberbully-5054.html   (AUG 28,2017)

11 Bass Anglers Against Bullying Presentation - Slideshare, https://www.slideshare.net/SteveGibson19/bass-anglers-against-bullying-presentat (accessed June 25, 2017)

12 Child Identity Theft: What Every Parent Needs to Know by Robert P. Chappell Jr. ISBN 978-1442218628 (AUG 1,2017)

13 Mother says daughter is victim of child identity theft ABC 10 (AUG 10, 2016) Retrieved from http://www.abc10. com/news/local/sacramento/mother-says-daughter-is-victim-of-child-identity-theft/310985336 (AUG 16, 2017)

14 Consumers Union's guide to security freeze protection (FEB, 5, 2014) Retrieved from http://consumersunion. org/research/consumers-unions-guide-to-security-freeze-protection/ (AUG 16,2017)

15 Your Access to Free Credit Reports." Federal Trade Commission. September 2005. Archived from the original on 21 December 2007. https://www.consumer.ftc.gov/ articles/0155-free-credit-reports (AUG 15, 2017)

16 Beware Of This Fake Snapchat Account Recruiting Teen Girls .., http://www.seventeen.com/life/news/a43717/ beware-of-this-fake-snapchat-account-r (accessed June 25, 2017)

17 : Police Probe Internet Scam Aimed At Teenage Girls - Newtown, https://newtownbee.com/police-probe-internet-scam-aimed-at-teenage-girls/ (accessed June 25, 2017).

18 Common Scams Targeted At Teens - Yahoo, https:// www.yahoo.com/news/common-scams-targeted-teens-213948601.html (accessed June 25, 2017).

19 China-based Fraudulent Prom Dress Websites Continue To .., http://www.prnewswire.com/news-releases/ china-based-fraudulent-prom-dress-websit es-continue-to-scam-american-teenage-girls-according-to-daphnedressescom-2508115 (accessed June 25, 2017).

20 Common Scams Targeted At Teens - Investopedia,

http://www.investopedia.com/financial-edge/1012/common-scams-targeted-at-teens.a (accessed June 25, 2017).

21 Family Fears Missing Ballantyne Teen Ran Off With Older .., http://www.cleveland19.com/story/32078064/family-fears-missing-ballantyne-teen-r (accessed June 25, 2017).

22 Warrants Detail Alleged Abuse Hailey Burns Endured While .., http://myfox8.com/2017/06/28/warrants-detail-alleged-abuse-hailey-burns-endured- (accessed June 25, 2017).

23 Preventing Identity Theft Jeff Lanza - Ctconstruction.org, http://www.ctconstruction.org/files/public/Lanza_HandOuts_11-2015.pdf (accessed June 25, 2017).

24 Snapchat Definition - Tech Terms, https://techterms.com/definition/snapchat (accessed June 25, 2017).

25 Family Educational Rights And Privacy Act (ferpa), http://www2.ed.gov/policy/gen/guid/fpco/ferpa/index.html (accessed June 25, 2017).

26 Protect Your Child's Data, Privacy At School: 5 Tips, http://www.creditcards.com/credit-card-news/protect-child-privacy-school-data-ti (accessed June 25, 2017).

27 Inbloom To Shut Down Amid Growing Data-privacy Concerns .., http://blogs.edweek.org/edweek/DigitalEducation/2014/04/inbloom_to_shut_down_ami (accessed June 25, 2017).

28 Efi Blog | Student Privacy 101: The Low Down On The Laws .., http://blog.educationframework.com/post/

student-privacy-101-the-low-down-on-the- (accessed June 25, 2017).

29 How Student Privacy And California's Sopipa ... - Cooley Go, https://www.cooleygo.com/how-student-privacy-and-californias-sopipa-may-affect-y (accessed June 25, 2017).

30 Notable New State Privacy And Data Security Laws – Part .., https://www.swlaw.com/blog/data-security/2017/02/20/notable-new-state-privacy-an (accessed June 25, 2017).

31 H.b. No. 7207 An Act Making Revisions To The Student Data, https://www.cga.ct.gov/2017/EDdata/Tmy/2017HB-07207-R000306-Connecticut%20Allian (accessed June 25, 2017).

32 World Privacy fourm opt out kids https://www.worldprivacyforum.org/optoutkids/ (accessed June 25, 2017).

33 Ferpa Model Notice For Directory Information, http://www2.ed.gov/policy/gen/guid/fpco/ferpa/mndirectoryinfo.html (accessed June 25, 2017).

34 In Turnaround, Judge Rules No Student Records To Be .., http://www.edweek.org/ew/articles/2016/03/16/in-turnaround-judge-rules-no-studen (accessed September 26, 2017).

35 Facebook® Accused Of Targeting 'insecure' Children And .., https://www.aol.com/article/finance/2017/05/01/Facebook®-accused-of-targeting-ins (accessed September 26, 2017).

36 Man Pleads Guilty For Selling Stealthgenie Spyware App And .., https://www.fbi.gov/contact-us/field-offices/washingtondc/news/press-releases/ma

n-pleads-guilty-for-selling-stealthgenie-spyware-app-and-ordered-to-pay-500-000- (accessed September 26, 2017).

37 Aaron's Law Reintroduced: Cfaa Didn't Fix Itself .., https://www.eff.org/deeplinks/2015/04/aarons-law-reintroduced-cfaa-didnt-fix-its (accessed September 26, 2017).

38 The Deep Web Vs. The Dark Web - Everything After Z By .., http://www.dictionary.com/e/dark-web/ (accessed September 26, 2017).

39 Schumer Pushes To Shut Down Online Drug Marketplace - Nbc .., http://www.nbcnewyork.com/news/local/Schumer-Calls-on-Feds-to-Shut-Down-Online-D (accessed September 26, 2017).

40 Silk Road Mastermind Ross Ulbricht Loses Legal Appeal, https://www.usatoday.com/story/money/2017/05/31/silk-road-mastermind-ross-ulbric (accessed September 26, 2017).

41 Tails - About, https://tails.boum.org/about/index.en.html (accessed September 26, 2017).

42 Can The Police See What I Google? | Yahoo Answers, https://answers.yahoo.com/question/index?qid=201006150 15707AAV1L7p (accessed September 26, 2017).

43 Copyright Trolls EFF https://www.eff.org/issues/

copyright-trolls (accessed September 26, 2017).

44 Ume Technology Committee - Wayne State, https://
www.med.wayne.edu/ume/files/2016/11/agenda_8-9-
16.pdf (accessed September 26, 2017).

45 An 18-Year-Old Girl Died From a Synthetic
Opioid She Bought Online. Here's How Portland Police
Cracked the Case. Willamette Week http://www.wweek.
com/news/2017/07/05/an-18-year-old-girl-died-from-a-
synthetic-opioid-she-bought-online-heres-how-portland-
police-cracked-the-case/

46 Self-harm | Nami: National Alliance On Mental
Illness, https://www.nami.org/Learn-More/Mental-Health-
Conditions/Related-Conditions/Self (accessed September
26, 2017).

47 Charged In Downtown Greenville Drug
Case, http://www.greenvilleonline.com/story/news/
crime/2017/04/27/2-charged-downtown-g (accessed
September 26, 2017).

48 A Modern Remake Of "your Brain On Drugs" : Videos,
https://www.reddit.com/r/videos/comments/66xvs5/a_
modern_remake_of_your_brain_on (accessed September
26, 2017).

49 How To Protect Your Child From Drug Abuse, http://
americanaddictioncenters.org/blog/5-ways-help-protect-
your-child-from-dru (accessed September 26, 2017).

50 10 Ways To Try To Prevent Drug Addiction In Your
Child .., http://www.parenting.com/child/health/10-ways-
to-try-to-prevent-drug-addiction-y (accessed September 26,

2017).

51 When Children View Pornography | Focus On The Family, http://www.focusonthefamily.com/parenting/ sexuality/when-children-use-pornograph (accessed September 26, 2017).

52 2017 Macmhp Conference - Leading The Way To Whole Person .., http://c.ymcdn.com/sites/www.macmhp. org/resource/resmgr/Events/SessionDetails_Tr (accessed September 26, 2017).

53 Star Guides Wilderness, Treatment Center, Pleasant Grove .., https://treatment.psychologytoday.com/rms/name/ Star+Guides+Wilderness_Pleasant+G (accessed September 26, 2017).

54 How Aaron Swartz Paved Way For Jack Andraka's .., http://www.vancouverobserver.com/world/how-aaron-swartz-paved-way-jack-andrakas- (accessed September 26, 2017).

55 12-year-old boy admits to hacking government sites for Anonymous The Verge https://www.theverge.com/20 13/10/26/5031718/12-year-old-boy-admits-to-hacking-government-sites-for-anonymous (accessed September 26, 2017).

56 Son Charges Dad's Credit Card for $8,000 on FIFA Microtransactions Gamerant Sarah Fields https://gamerant. com/8000-fifa-microtransactions-charge/ (accessed September 26, 2017).

57 'surprised And Delighted' Ontario Dad Gets Full

Refund   For   ..,   http://globalnews.ca/news/2476491/
surprised-and-delighted-ontario-dad-gets-full-   (accessed
September 26, 2017).

58 Google Settles With Ftc Over In-app Charges - Phys.
org, https://phys.org/news/2014-09-google-ftc-in-app.html
(accessed September 26, 2017).

59 Kid Racks Up $5,900 Bill Playing Jurassic World On
Dad's ... (n.d.). Retrieved from https://games.slashdot.org/
story/16/01/03/1438235/kid-racks-up-5900-bill-playing

Chicago: Kid   Racks   Up $5,900   Bill   Playing
Jurassic World On Dad's .., https://games.slashdot.org/
story/16/01/03/1438235/kid-racks-up-5900-bill-playing
(accessed September 26, 2017).

60 2010 July - Bits - The New York Times, https://bits.
blogs.nytimes.com/2010/07/   (accessed   September   26,
2017).

61 Marvel Avengers Alliance 1, 2 Shutting Down Isn't
A .., http://www.product-reviews.net/2016/09/01/marvel-
avengers-alliance-1-2-shutting-   (accessed   September   26,
2017).

62 Mobile Game Revenue To Pass Console, Pc For First
Time,   https://www.cnbc.com/2016/04/22/mobile-game-
revenue-to-pass-console-pc-for-first (accessed September 26,
2017).

63 Federal Trade Commission, https://www.ftc.gov/sites/
default/files/documents/federal_register_notices/child
            rens-online-privacy-protection-rule-16-cfr-part-
312/990427childrensonlineprivacy (accessed September 26,

2017).

64 Archer Hayes Et Al V. Toytalk, Inc. Et Al (2:16-cv-02111   .., https://www.pacermonitor.com/public/case/11081356/Archer_Hayes_et_al_v_ToyTalk,_ (accessed September 26, 2017).

65 : 'google Home' Voice Activated Digital Assistant Video .., http://abcnews.go.com/Technology/video/google-home-voice-activated-digital-assis (accessed September 26, 2017).

66 Mattel Built A $300 Echo For Kids - Engadget, https://live.engadget.com/2017/01/03/mattel-aristotle-echo-speaker-kids/ (accessed September 26, 2017).

67 http://news.sky.com/story/blue-whale-death-game-leaves-a-trail-of-misery-for-russian-families-10942187

68 The Deadliest Dose: Treating The National Opioid Epidemic   .., https://blog.getmeadow.com/the-deadliest-dose-treating-the-national-opioid-epide (accessed September 26, 2017).

69 Prescription Drug Abuse Statistics - Bayside Marin, http://www.baysidemarin.com/prescription-drugs/abuse-statistics/ (accessed September 26, 2017).

70 Encryption Vs. Cryptography - What Is The Difference?, http://www.brighthub.com/computing/enterprise-security/articles/65254.aspx (accessed September 26, 2017).

71 Simple Transposition Ciphers - Crypto Corner, http://crypto.interactive-maths.com/simple-transposition-ciphers.html (accessed September 26, 2017).

72 Flaws In Ss7 Protocol Allow Hackers To Spy On Phone

.., http://securityaffairs.co/wordpress/31262/hacking/flaws-ss7-protocol-spy-on-phon (accessed September 26, 2017).

73 Harvard Rescinds Admissions To 10 Students For ... - Forbes, https://www.forbes.com/sites/rebeccaheilweil1/2017/06/05/harvard-rescinds-10-adm issions-offer-for-offensive-Facebook®-memes-ollowing-commencement-speaker-zuckerb (accessed September 26, 2017).

74 8 Fascinating Facts About How Teens Use The Internet And Social Media Carly Steyer http://www.huffingtonpost.com/entry/tk-facts-about-teens-on-social-media-that-are-really-scary_us_55a7c6f0e4b0896514d06eab (accessed September 26, 2017).

75 College Admission: The Complete Guide to Social Media - Kaplan test prep https://www.kaptest.com/study/college-admissions/college-admission-the-complete-guide-to-social-media/ (accessed September 26, 2017).

76 Social Media and Recruiting: 5 Things Every HR Leader Should Know https://www.adp.com/spark/articles/social-media-and-recruiting-5-things-every-hr-leader-should-know-7-963.aspx

77 Tips To Preserve Your Digital Reputation This Summer, https://www.fosi.org/good-digital-parenting/tips-preserve-your-digital-reputatio (accessed September 26, 2017).

78 http://www.nytimes.com/2013/11/10/business/they-loved-your-gpa-then-they-saw-your-tweets.html

Glossary

A

Abuse The misuse of any intoxicant drugs or alcohol and the habitual taking of addictive or illegal drugs, compounds that distort accepted reality.

Addiction A condition of being dependent on a particular substance, thing, or activity

Advertising The activity or profession of producing announcements for commercial products or services

AI An acronym for Artificial Intelligence the theory and development of computer systems able to perform tasks that normally require human intelligence, such as visual perception, speech recognition, decision-making, and translation between languages.

AlphaBay A site on the dark web that operated similarly to eBay that was raided for selling illegal drugs and anything else that is deemed forbidden by civilized society.

American Express A membership driven card and service that provides a service that is the most respected throughout the world.

Android An open source operating system introduced by Google and supported by millions of developers throughout the world. It is found running phones, tablets and computers branded with the Google name.

Apple An American computer company that is the developer of cutting edged designed products, which include the IPhone8 and Mac (Macintosh) Macbook, MiniMac, etc..

Avengers Alliance A property of Marvel comics and a video game produced by Playdom that ran on the Facebook game platform.

B

Banking industry A group of powerful people that control the destiny of the uper 1% and the lives of the other 99%.

Big data It is generally it is a large set of data with millions of records. Often it includes records that have been stolen or the result of spying or misinforming the general public of its intended use.

Bookbaby An internet-based publishing and distribution company that assists authors with the distribution of primarily eBook formatted material. It also has the ability to print-on-demand copies of physical books.

Brand loyalty It is the tendency of some consumers to continue buying the same brand of goods rather than competing brands.

Browser A program that translates various script languages to display them for a user. The most popular ones in use today are Firefox, Chrome, Opera, Safari, Internet Explorer and Microsoft Edge.

Browser history a list of websites visited by a web browser.

C

Cell phone A portable bugging device that most Americans carry around with them.

Chex Systems A bank enforcement company and a listed regulated credit reporting company

Child pornography it is still pictures or video of anyone under the age of 18 naked in any form or engaged in or suggesting the engagement of sexually suggestive poses. On a computer is can also be a file name or a fragment of a computer.

Children's Online Privacy Protection Act A law passed by Congress that is really outdated and needs updating with stronger enforcement that should protect children online no matter what site they are on.

Cocaine A lucrative and illegal drug in an illegal business model that bypasses all efforts of society and its law enforcement to make billions of dollars of profits every year in the black market.

College admissions offices The office where the decisions are made of who can attend a particular college or university.

Confidence games or a Con game By using illicit motivates separating someone else from something of value by use of trickery, deceit or fraud

COPPA It is acronym for the Children's Online Privacy Protection Act

Corporate manipulation The act of trickery or deceit to entice someone into an action or to purchase a product or service based on a fictional want or need.

CreateSpace An internet-based publishing and distribution company that assists authors with the distribution of primarily eBook formatted material. It also has the ability to print-on-demand copies of physical books.

Credit card A Method to add fees to merchants and gain interest from consumers for purchasing any good or service.

Credit card bill The invoice that details everything that happened at the end of the month except who the company sold the information to.

Credit card companies are organizations that have the sole purpose to enslave its cardholder into the burden of debt.

Credit card information It includes the card number, expiration date, name, and cvv or cvt code. All of the information is on the chip or magnetic strip attached to the physical card except the code. On American Express card, the code is on the front

Credit card provider It is the company that issues someone a credit card and sends the bill to the consumer

Credit card system Every aspect of the credit industry including issuing banks, merchant banks, and providers

Credit card theft A problem that is not had to fix if the industry really wanted to fix it.

Credit card transaction A description of what of occurs when a credit card is used in lieu of a cash transaction.

Credit system See **Credit card system**

Cyber-attack An attempt by hackers working independently or with criminals or governments military to damage or destroy a computer network or system.

Cyberbully People who are intent to destroy and hide behind a computer to terrorize someone else .

Cybercrime An act of using the internet to steal information by an individual, criminal gang or corporation see data broker

Cyber predator A person who is a criminal that hunts for victims using a computer

Cybersecurity An overused word describing a combination of a firewall and network tools to detect, block and remediate a network intrusion.

Cybertipline A website operated by the National Center for Missing and Exploited Children

D

Data Broker A company that sells personal information to anyone. An example is the credit reporting industry. Some buy stolen information and are directly responsible for identiy theft.

Darknet If you can understand the internet contains webpages then the dark web is on the darknet.

Dark Web It is part of the darknet where privacy exists with Tor and a few others

Date of birth One of keys of your identity that you should never put on the internet.

Debian An operating system in the Linux family More stable than Windows and a cousin to Apple os.

Debit card A card that looks identical to a credit card but offers virtually no protection

Deep Web A description of the internet and all things connected to it

Department of Homeland Security A combination of investigative departments of the United States Federal Government.

Designer drug Typical it is chemicals that are produced to consume by humans that is really a poison to the brain to make the person feel different most are extremely toxic.

Device security It refers to anything that connects to the internet and is used by children. It could include a game system, tablet, smartphone or computer.

Disney A multi-billion-dollar a year company that specializes in entrainment and invented the idea of selling matching merchandise in movies to children's parents.

Disneyesque Anything resembling or suggestive of the films, television productions, or amusement parks made by Walt Disney or his organization

Drug Any substance which has a physiological effect when ingested or otherwise introduced into the body.

Drug abuse The habitual use of a drug

Drug addict or **Drug-addicted** or **Drug addiction** It is a chronic, relapsing brain disease that is characterized by compulsive drug seeking and use, despite harmful consequences. It is considered a brain disease because drugs change the brain; they change its structure and how it works.

Drug culture The social acceptance of taking drugs as an acceptable exercise.

Drug deal A description of a transaction where something of value is traded for an illegal substance

Drug dealer Someone who trades or buys any sort of drug and in doing so creates a profit

Drug epidemic It is the rapid increase in the use of prescription and non-prescription drugs

Drug overdose The effect of the body as it attempts to shut down after taking poison.

Drug rehabilitation is the processes of medical or psychotherapeutic treatment for dependency on psychoactive substances.

Drug trade A description of a market that spans the globe buying and selling illegal intoxicants

Drug trafficking A legal description of the drug trade

E

Electronic Arts A company that creates video games

EA sports Formerly a marketing gimmick of Electronic Arts, in which they tried to imitate real-life sports networks by calling themselves the "EA Sports Network"

eBay A website that allows buys and sellers to exchange things of perceived value for money

Email These are messages distributed by electronic means from one computer user to one or more recipients via an unsecured medium. Never send anything confidential without encryption.

Equifax One of the oldest consumer spies that invented the business of selling personal information it was recently hacked and lost undisclosed amounts of personal information. It is also a regulated credit reporting organization.

Experian A data broker sells information that should be covered und HIPPA it is also a regulated credit reporting organization.

F

Facebook A Social media site run by hackers with a website that monitors users actions and summarizes posted material sells it to a broker it also has the world's largest index of faces with names. It also tracks users locations 24/7, and it tracks web activity of anyone

Federal authorities The FBI, Homeland security or any agency that is in law enforcement at the federal level

Federal Trade Commission An agency in the federal government that can only use the court to enforce regulation

G

Game card Another form of converting physical money into virtual tokens for imaginary things of value

Game console A minicomputer designed for playing video games

Game crack A software application or process that removes limitations or the requirement for registration or a serial number to operate. In short it is a great way to get a virus.

Game currency The invention of turning real money into imaginary benefit

Game developer A programmer, analyst or phycologist who works to create additive video games.

Game engine It is a framework by which a game can be built without writing the whole thing. It's like an operating system in a way.

Game industry A sector exchange-traded fund that invests solely in gaming companies,

Game platform A computer system specially made for playing video games. It is also called a console:

Gamers The name that was given to describe people who obsessively play video games

GNU/Linux It is an operating system. GNU is a recursive acronym for "GNU's Not Unix!", chosen because GNU's design is Unix-like, but differs from Unix by being free software and containing no Unix code. The GNU project includes an operating system kernel, GNU HURD, which was the original focus of the Free Software Foundation (FSF)

Google A multi-billion-dollar company that is part of the Alphabet corporation

Google advertising It redefined the internet and it model of advertising selling links because of it popularity.

Google AdWords The process of renting keywords that other people search for to solicit advertising for a product or service

Google Hangouts A product of Goole that turns any device with a microphone and speakers into a phone with incoming and outgoing calls (video or audio only) and SMS(text) messages it competes with Microsoft skype platform

Google Images An index of images that were collected by its crawling across the internet each owned by somone else.

Google Play Store A place to download for purchase or free media, movies, games, books, application or enhancements to Google products, for example, the android phone or the Chrome web browser

Google Trends A web page that shows how many people used google to look up something by any keyword or group of keywords over time.

GPS The Global positioning system. There are 3 sets of satellites that provide the same information they are owned individually by Russia, China, and the United States.

Gunrunner Someone who transports illegal guns or other munitions for sale

H

Hansa Market A dark web marketplace that was raided by international authorities led by the FBI and operated to trap buyers and sellers.

Hardcore pornography A type of pornography outside of reality and not showing love or respect for another person.

Heroin A illicit drug that comes primarily from Afghanistan

Hollywood A city in California where the glorification of narcissists is normalized.

I

Information gathering The act of collecting what otherwise would be benign esoteric pieces of information.

Internet filter A device or software program that blocks words or site content

Internet porn Is sexually explicit content made available online. porn sites receive more hits during business hours than at other times of the day. According to AVN magazine, a trade publication that tracks the adult video industry.

Internet scam It is a term used to describe any fraudulent business or scheme that defrauds an unsuspecting person.

 IOS an operating system used for mobile devices manufactured by Apple Inc.

IP address A unique string of numbers that is the basis for communicating on the internet.

IPhone A Combination portable computer and phone which began the smartphone revolution mad by Apple Inc.

J

Junk mail Things that you don't want that was sent to your home that was caused by the data broker industry

Jurassic World It is a mobile simulation game made by the game developers: Ludia. That runs on IOS and Android

Just for marketing A myth to justify spying and stealing peoples personal data and habits.

K

K9 security Is proprietary software which is free for home use. It is possible to have multiple licenses, and every computer needs a separate license. Its primary purpose is for parental control, but it is possible to use it for protection of their computer against computer viruses or malware, or for self-blocking of pornography

L

Law enforcement Is any system by which some members of society act in an organized manner to enforce the law

M

Mac The Macintosh (branded as Mac since 1998) is a series of personal computers (PCs) designed, developed, and marketed by Apple Inc. Steve Jobs introduced the original Macintosh computer on January 24, 1984

Malware Any program or app installed on a computer or device that does things that the owner is not aware of and can be as malicious as a virus

Manipulation The act of convincing someone to do an act or to believe that they want or need something that they don', It is commonly used in marketing

Marvel Avengers Alliance was a turn-based social network game developed by Offbeat Creations and published by Playdom on March 1, 2012. It was based on characters and storylines published by Marvel Comics;.

MasterCard A credit, charge, debit or prepaid card branded by MasterCard Incorporated

Methamphetamines A synthetic drug with more rapid and lasting effects than amphetamine used illegally as a stimulant

Microsoft A global corporation that dominates the computer industry

Microtransaction A method to trick users into paying what seems like small insignificant amounts

Mobile device Any device that uses batteries instead of directly plugging into a home power outlet.

Monitoring It isto observe and check the progress or quality of (something) over a period of time

MPAA An acronym for The Motion Picture Association of America it is a film rating system and powerful lobbying organization that enforces copyright violations

MySpace is a social networking website offering an interactive, user-submitted network of friends that has been plagued with viruses hacked more times than any another in the history of the internet

N

National Cyber Security Alliance a 501c(3) nonprofit founded in 2001, is the United States' leading public-private partnership promoting cybersecurity, privacy education and awareness.

Newspaper A term for news when it was printed on paper and there were real investigative reporters. Now there are just people spreading rumour's on the internet.

O

Online A term to describe any device with access to the internet or any other network

Online address An internet address of a device see Ip address

Online contact One person having communication with someone else using the internet

Online database a store of information about subjects in this case, however, it is mostly stolen information

Online game A game that can only be played while connected to the internet usually on a website

Online transactions The act of transferring something of perceived value to someone else using the internet as a method of communication

Online world A description of social media and its effects on the people who use it.

P

Pay-to-win In some players who are willing to pay for special items or downloadable content may be able to gain a significant advantage over those playing for free. Some critics of such games call them "pay-to-win" or "p2w" games.

PayPal A Ebay company that acts as a bank but is not regulated like one. Often it is used to transfer money for objects of perceived value

Pedophile A person who is sexually attracted to children Personal computer IX

Pink See **U-47700**

Pirated game A game that was copied without a proper transaction or valid ownership.

Porn see **Pornographic**

Porn Hub It is a pornographic video sharing website on the internet. It claims to be the largest pornographic site.

Pornographic Any image or sound that depicts sexuality that is displeasing to the general in public

Pornography it is printed or visual material containing the explicit description or display of sexual organs or activity,

Porn sites See **Porn website**

Porn statistics It is the storage of users actions on a porn site to gather data about user actions or equipment used to connect to a porn site

Porn website A website that contains Pornography

Predator A person or group that ruthlessly exploits others.

Privacy It is the act of being left (let) alone and not being bothered by any outside influence or act. Its orgins are base in common law.

Prostitutes A description of someone who sells their body to engage in sexual actions in exchange for money

Psychological research It refers to investigations that psychologists use to conduct and analyze the experiences and behaviors of individuals or groups

Puppy video Cute videos that people post online there are ones that feature cats as well.

PVP A term in the video game industry to describe players playing against other players

R

RIAA An acronym for the Recording Industry Association of America it is an organization that represents the music recording industry's intellectual property rights. The organization has taken an especially aggressive stance against Internet users who want to be able to freely copy published music.

Router A router is a networking device that forwards data packets between computer networks

S

Scam A dishonest scheme; a fraud

Scam artist A person who attempts to defraud others by presenting a fraudulent offer and pretending that it is legitimate

Scambusters An organization that has helped over eleven million people protect themselves from scams since November 1994.

Scammer See **scam artist**

Security The state of being free from danger or threat.

Security firm A company that specializes in selling security to others

Sexting The process of sending or receiving pornographic images through the cell phone network using SMS (text) messaging

Shaping your child's ideas Corporations or people who attempt to persuade or give your child an idea that is outside of your belief system

Silk Road It was at its time the largest bust of a dark website in history. Its prosecution of its suspected founder left many in the tech industry baffled. It was a media circus

Sir Tim Berners-Lee The inventor of the World Wide Web

Smashwords An internet-based publishing and distribution company that assists authors with the distribution of primarily eBook formatted material. It also has the ability to do print on demand of physical books.

Snapchat A mobile messaging service from Snap Inc. that sends a photo or video to someone; it lasts only up to 10 seconds before it disappears. During that time, the recipient can take a screenshot, and the sender is notified that it was taken.

Social game A video game that is played with others generally on a social network

Social influence It occurs when a person's emotions, opinions, or behaviors are affected by others.

Social network A dedicated website or other application that enables users to communicate with each other by posting information, comments, messages, images, etc.

Social Security A United States Federal program of social insurance and benefits developed in 1935. The Social Security program's benefits include retirement income, disability income, Medicare and Medicaid, as well as death and survivorship benefits.

Social Security Administration It is an independent agency of the U.S. federal government that administers Social Security,

Social Security Card A card issued by the government that has a identification number on it that is used for credit insurance and other things it was never intended for.

Sony A international conglomerate based in Japan that owns many divisions including entrainment, movie production, and a video game system

Spam unwanted emails

Spammers Someone who buys your email address from a Data Broker and send you junk you don't want.

Spying The act of observing people without their knowledge

Spyware a program designed to steal your information; it is not a crime like hacking because a data broker wrote it

State security It is Federal Government agencies that require secure communication state department, the State Department, and CIA

SWAT In the United States, SWAT (Special Weapons And Tactics) is a law enforcement unit which uses specialized or military equipment and tactics.

T

Tablet An enclosed computer with a touchscreen interface that runs off of batteries

Television An antique device that carried entertainment and news before the internet and computers

The Direct Marketing Association A lobby organization that is promoted as a self-regulatory solution to stealing and selling personal data

Thumb drive A chip with a USB connection to store computer data. It is also called a flash drive.

TransUnion A data broker that sells lists and pictures of your car when it encounters a traffic camera.

Twitter An online news and social networking service where users post and interact with messages, "tweets" and is restricted to 140 characters.

U

U-47700 A designer drug mostly made in China that is available on the dark web.

U.S. Senator Chuck Schumer He was first elected in 1981 and a prime example of a lifetime politician.

U.S. Food and Drug Administration (FDA or USFDA) is a federal agency of the United States Department of Health and Human Services, one of the United States federal executive departments.

V

Virtual item Things that do not really exist.

Virus A piece of code that is capable of copying itself and typically has a detrimental effect, such as corrupting the system or destroying data.

Visa A credit, debit or prepaid card branded by Visa Inc., a major payments technology company.

W

War Games Is a 1983 American Cold War science fiction film about, a young hacker who unwittingly accesses WOPR (War Operation Plan Response), a United States military supercomputer; it was originally programmed to predict possible outcomes of nuclear war.

Warlord A military commander, especially an aggressive regional commander with individual autonomy and not part of civilized recognized government.

Web site A server that hosts web pages

Wi-Fi A technology using radio signals allowing computers, smartphones, or other devices to connect to the Internet or communicate with one another wirelessly within a particular area.

Windows A computer operating system with a graphical user interface.

X

Xbox A popular video game console from Microsoft. Introduced in 2001, the Xbox was designed to compete with Sony's PlayStation and Nintendo's GameCube.

Y

Yahoo A Web directory developed in the early 1990s by Stanford graduate students David Filo and Jerry Yang. Yahoo! has expanded into a full-featured Web portal, including a search engine, chat groups, instant messaging (IM), and e-mail.

Z

Zanyga A video game producer that uses Facebook primarily as a delivery platform

Index

H

I

J

K

L

M

CPSIA information can be obtained
at www.ICGtesting.com
Printed in the USA
BVOW09s0132061017
496831BV00003B/3/P